The Really Useful

Home Book

"What's in a name? That which we call a rose
By any other name would smell as sweet."

Shakespeare (Romeo & Juliet)

A Robert Frederick Gift Book

The Really Useful Home Book

A compendium of facts, figures and useful information

INDEX

ITEM	PAGE NO.

INDEX

PERSONAL NOTES

Name ....

Address ....

Tel.: Home ....

Business ....

Car ....

In Case of Emergency

Contact ....

Telephone No. ....

Blood Group ....

Known Allergies ....

❖ Useful Telephone Numbers

Accountant ....

Airport ....

Bank ....

Building Society ....

Club ....

Dentist ....

Doctor ....

Electrician ....

Gas ....

Optician ....

Plumber ....

Railway Station ....

Solicitor ....

Taxi/Car Hire ....

Travel Agent ....

Vet ....

Water ....

Other ....

❖ Useful Information

National Insurance No. ....

Passport No. ....

Driving Licence No. ....

Credit Card No.s ....

Car Key No. ....

Car Insurance Policy No. ....

Renewal Date ....

AA/RAC Membership No. ....

❖ Notes

....

....

....

USEFUL TELEPHONE NUMBERS

Name ☎
Name ☎
Name ☎
Name ☎
Name ☎
Name ☎
Name ☎
Name ☎
Name ☎
Name ☎
Name ☎
Name ☎
Name ☎
Name ☎
Name ☎
Name ☎
Name ☎
Name ☎
Name ☎
Name ☎
Name ☎
Name ☎
Name ☎

THINGS TO REMEMBER

Use this space to note down renewal dates for Television Licence, Road Tax, MOT, Insurance policies etc.

BIRTH SIGNS

ARIES (March 21-April 20)
Fiery First Sign
Symbol: The Ram
Ruling Planet: Mars
Birthstone: Diamond
Flower: Sweet Pea
Colours: Fiery Red, Orange
Numbers: Seven, Six
Day: Tuesday

TAURUS (April 21-May 21)
Earthy Second Sign
Symbol: The Bull
Ruling Planet: Venus
Birthstone: Emerald
Flower: Lily of the Valley
Colours: Natural colours
Numbers: One, Nine
Day: Friday

GEMINI (May 22-June 21)
Airy Third Sign
Symbol: The Twins
Ruling Planet: Mercury
Birthstone: Agate
Flower: Rose
Colours: Sky Blue, Black
Numbers: Three, Four
Day: Wednesday

CANCER (June 22-July 22)
Watery Fourth Sign
Symbol: Crab, Moon
Ruling Planet: The Moon
Birthstone: Moonstone, Pearl
Flower: Larkspur
Colours: Silver, Sea Green
Numbers: Eight, Three
Day: Friday

LEO (July 23-August 23)
Fiery & Fixed Fifth Sign
Symbol: The Sun, The Lion
Ruling Planet: The Sun
Birthstone: Sardonyx
Flower: Gladioli
Colours: Gold, Fiery Shades
Numbers: Five, Nine
Day: Sunday

VIRGO (August 24-Sept. 22)
Earthy & Adaptable Sixth Sign
Symbol: Fertility Goddess
Ruling Planet: Mercury
Birthstone: Sapphire
Flower: Aster
Colours: Natural, Warm
Numbers: Eight, Four
Day: Wednesday

LIBRA (Sept. 23-Oct. 23)
Airy Sociable Seventh Sign
Symbol: The Scales
Ruling Planet: Venus
Birthstone: Opal
Flower: Calendula
Colour: Peacock Blue
Numbers: Six, Nine
Day: Friday

SCORPIO (Oct. 24-Nov. 22)
Watery Eighth Sign
Symbol: The Scorpion
Ruling Planet: Mars
Birthstone: Topaz
Flower: Chrysanthemum
Colours: Dark Water Shades
Numbers: Three, Five
Day: Tuesday

SAGITTARIUS (Nov. 23-Dec. 23)
Fiery, Adaptable Ninth Sign
Symbol: The Archer
Ruling Planet: Jupiter
Birthstone: Turquoise
Flower: Narcissus
Colours: Fiery Reds
Number: Nine
Day: Thursday

CAPRICORN (Dec. 24-Jan. 20)
Earthy Tenth Sign
Symbol: The Goat
Ruling Planet: Saturn
Birthstone: Garnet
Flower: Carnation
Colours: Restrained to Dark
Numbers: Seven, Three
Day: Saturday

AQUARIUS (Jan. 21-Feb. 18)
Airy, Stubborn Eleventh Sign
Symbol: Water Carrier
Ruling Planet: Uranus
Birthstone: Amethyst
Flower: Violet
Colours: Wild, Way Out
Numbers: Eight, Four
Day: Wednesday

PISCES (Feb. 19-March 20)
Watery, Compromising Twelfth Sign
Symbol: Two Fish
Ruling Planet: Neptune
Birthstone: Bloodstone
Flower: Jonquil
Colours: Violet, Oceanic
Numbers: Five, Eight
Day: Friday

BIRTHDAYS

Spouse ....

Children ....

....

....

....

....

Grandchildren

....

....

....

....

....

....

....

Mother ....

Father ....

Mother-in-law ....

Father-in-law ....

Brothers & Sisters

....

....

....

....

....

....

Other Family

....

....

....

....

....

....

Friends

....

....

....

....

....

....

....

Miscellaneous

....

....

....

....

....

....

....

ANNIVERSARIES

"It is not the years in your life but the life in your years that counts!"

Adlai Stevenson: Coronet

~ WEDDING ANNIVERSARIES ~

First	Paper	Tenth	Tin	Thirtieth	Pearl
Second	Cotton	Eleventh	Steel	Thirty-fifth	Coral
Third	Leather	Twelfth	Silk, Linen	Forty-fifth	Sapphire
Fourth	Fruit, Flowers	Thirteenth	Lace	Fortieth	Ruby
Fifth	Wood	Fourteenth	Ivory	Fiftieth	Gold
Sixth	Sugar, Iron	Fifteenth	Crystal	Fifty-fifth	Emerald
Seventh	Wool, Copper	Twentieth	China	Sixtieth	Diamond
Eighth	Bronze, Pottery	Twenty-fifth	Silver	Seventieth	Platinum
Ninth	Pottery, Willow			Seventy-fifth	Diamond

SPECIAL OCCASIONS

Occasion .... Date ....

Occasion .... Date ....

Occasion .... Date ....

Occasion .... Date ....

Occasion .... Date ....

Occasion .... Date ....

Occasion .... Date ....

Occasion .... Date ....

Occasion .... Date ....

Occasion .... Date ....

Occasion .... Date ....

Occasion .... Date ....

Occasion .... Date ....

"All who joy would win
Must share it, -
Happiness was born a Twin."

Byron: Don Juan

QUOTATIONS FOR SPECIAL OCCASIONS

Absence/Parting

"Sometimes when one person
is missing, the whole world
seems depopulated."

Lamartine

"To leave is to die a little;
It is to die to what one loves.
One leaves behind a little of oneself
At any hour, any place."

Edmond Haraucourt

"The joys of meeting pay
the pangs of absence;
Else who could bear it?"

Nicholas Rowe

Bereavement

"Pain lays not its touch
Upon a corpse."

Aeschylus

"He who has gone, so we but
cherish his memory, abides with us,
more potent, nay, more present,
than the living man."

Saint-Exupéry

Births

"We find delight in the beauty
and happiness of children
that makes the heart too big
for the body."

Ralph Waldo Emerson

"Children are poor men's riches."

English Proverb

"There never was child so lovely
but his mother was glad to
get him asleep."

Ralph Waldo Emerson

"Life's aspirations come in the
guise of children."

Rabindranath Tagore

"Adam and Eve had many
advantages but the principal one
was that they escaped teething."

Mark Twain

"A sweet child is the sweetest
thing in nature."

Charles Lamb

EVERYDAY THOUGHTS
for everyday living

"They are able because
they think they are able."

Virgil

"Natural ability without education
has oftener raised men to glory
and virtue, than education without
natural ability."

Cicero

"Our hours in love have wings;
in absence crutches."

Colley Cibber

"Absence diminishes moderate
passions and increases great ones,
as the wind extinguishes tapers and
adds fury to fire."

François de la Rochefoucauld

"He knows not his own strength
that hath not met adversity."

Ben Jonson

Addresses • Addresses • Addresses • Addresses • Addresses • Addresses • Addresses

A

Name

Name

Name

Name

Name

Name

Birthdays

"First you forget names, then you forget faces, then you forget to pull your zipper up, then you forget to pull your zipper down."

Lee Rosenburg

"Whenever a man's friends begin to compliment him about looking young, he may be sure that they think he is growing old."

Washington Irving

"Unto each man comes a day when his favourite sins all forsake him, And he complacently thinks he has forsaken his sins."

John Hay

"How beautiful is youth!
how bright it gleams
With its illusions, aspirations, dreams."

Longfellow

"It's not that age brings childhood back again, Age merely shows what children we remain."

Goethe: Faust

Birthdays

"What [Time] hath scanted men in hair, he hath given them in wit."

Shakespeare: The Comedy of Errors

"It isn't how long you stick around but what you put over while you are here."

George Ade

"Middle age is when your age starts to show around the middle."

Bob Hope

"To me, old age is always fifteen years older than I am."

Bernard Baruch

"Old men like to give good advice in order to console themselves for not being any longer able to set bad examples."

François de la Rochefoucauld

"Growing old is no more than a bad habit which a busy man has no time to form."

André Maurois

EVERYDAY THOUGHTS
for everyday living

"There is nothing which we receive with so much reluctance as advice."

Joseph Addison

"Age only matters when one is aging. Now that I have arrived at a great age. I might just as well be twenty."

Picasso

"Aim at the sun, and you may not reach it; but your arrow will fly far higher than if aimed at an object on a level with yourself."

J Hawes

"He that is slow to anger is better than the mighty; and he that ruleth his spirit than he that taketh a city."

Proverbs 16:32

"The only way to get the best of an argument is to avoid it."

Dale Carnegie

Addresses • Addresses • Addresses • Addresses • Addresses • Addresses • Addresses

A

Name

✉

☎

Name

✉

☎

Name

✉

☎

Name

✉

☎

Name

✉

☎

Name

✉

☎

QUOTATIONS FOR SPECIAL OCCASIONS

CONSOLATION

"Let us remember, when we are inclined to be disheartened, that the private soldier is a poor judge of the fortunes of a great battle."

W R Inge

"It's not how far you fall, but how high you bounce."

Author Unidentified

"When the One Great Scorer comes to write against your name, He marks, not that you won or lost, but how you played the game."

Grantland Rice

COURAGE

"Don't be afraid to take big steps. You can't cross a chasm in two small jumps."

David Lloyd George

"What matters is not the size of the dog in the fight, but the size of the fight in the dog."

Coach Bear Bryant

DIFFICULT TIMES

"Human misery must somewhere have a stop: there is no wind that always blows a storm."

Euripides

"God will not look you over for medals, degrees or diplomas, but for scars."

Elbert Hubbard

"The worse the passage the more welcome the port."

Thomas Fuller

EDUCATION

"An investment in knowledge always pays the best interest."

Benjamin Franklin

"Education is an ornament in prosperity and a refuge in adversity."

Aristotle

"Learning without thought is labour lost; thought without learning is perilous."

Confucius

EVERYDAY THOUGHTS
for everyday living

"Every baby born into the world
is a finer one than the last."

Charles Dickens: Nicholas Nickleby

"A baby is an angel whose wings
decrease as his legs increase."

French Proverb

" A beautiful face is of all spectacles
the most beautiful."

Jean de la Bruyère

"Achieving starts with believing."

Author Unidentified

"A man lives by believing something:
not by debating and arguing
about many things."

Thomas Carlyle

Addresses • Addresses • Addresses • Addresses • Addresses • Addresses • Addresses

B

Name

✉

☎

Name

✉

☎

Name

✉

☎

Name

✉

☎

Name

✉

☎

Name

✉

☎

Family

"To forget one's ancestors is to be
a brook without a source,
a tree without a root."

Chinese Proverb

"When brothers agree, no fortress
is so strong as their common life."

Antisthenes

"God could not be everywhere,
so He made mothers."

Jewish Proverb

"Mother is the name for God in the
lips and hearts of little children."

W M Thackeray: Vanity Fair

"When I was a boy of fourteen, my
father was so ignorant I could hardly
stand to have the old man around.
But when I got to be twenty one,
I was astonished at how much
he had learned in seven years."

Mark Twain

"A father is a banker by nature."

French Proverb

Friendship

"There's nothing worth
the wear of winning,
But laughter and the
love of friends."

Hilaire Belloc

"A friend may well be reckoned
the masterpiece of nature."

Ralph Waldo Emerson

"We do not mind our not arriving
anywhere nearly so much as our not
having any company on the way."

Frank Moore Colby

Happiness

"Silence is the perfectest herald
of joy. I were but little happy if
I could say how much."

Shakespeare: Much Ado About Nothing

"Grief can take care of itself,
but to get the full value of joy
you must have somebody to
divide it with."

~ Mark Twain

EVERYDAY THOUGHTS
for everyday living

"Burdens become light when
cheerfully borne."

Author Unidentified

"Whenever you see a successful
business, someone once made
a courageous decision."

Peter Drucker

"To business that we love
we rise betime,
And go to't with delight."

Shakespeare: Anthony and Cleopatra

"Few people do business well
who do nothing else."

Lord Chesterfield

"The busier we are, the more acutely
we feel that we live, the more
conscious we are of life."

Immanuel Kant

Addresses • Addresses • Addresses • Addresses • Addresses • Addresses • Addresses

B

Name

Name

Name

Name

Name

Name

QUOTATIONS FOR SPECIAL OCCASIONS

House-Warming

"You are a king by your own fire-side, as much as any monarch in his throne."

Cervantes

"A man's home is his wife's castle."

Alexander Chase

Love

"Love, all alike, no season knows,
nor clime,
Nor hours, age, months,
which are the rags of time."

John Donne

"One word
Frees us of all the weight
and pain of life:
That word is love."

Sophocles

"All love is sweet,
Given or returned.
Common as light is love,
And its familiar voice wearies
not ever."

Shelley

Retirement

"Cessation of work is not accompanied by cessation of expenses."

Cato the Elder

"Dismiss the old horse in good time, lest he fail in the lists and the spectators laugh."

Horace

"To the art of working well a civilised race would add the art of playing well."

George Santayana

Reunions

"A man's real possession is his memory. In nothing else is he rich, in nothing else is he poor."

Alexander Smith

"To be able to enjoy one's past life is to live twice."

Martial

"Bliss in possession will not last;
Remembered joys are never past."

James Montgomery

EVERYDAY THOUGHTS
for everyday living

"Challenges can be stepping stones or stumbling blocks. It's just a matter of how you view them."

Author Unidentified

"Wondrous is the strength of cheerfulness, and its power of endurance - the cheerful man will do more in the same time, will do it better, will persevere in it longer than the sad or sullen."

Thomas Carlyle

"Of cheerfulness, or a good temper - the more it is spent, the more of it remains."

Ralph Waldo Emerson

"Children are the true connoisseurs. What's precious to them has no price, only value."

Bel Kaufman

Addresses • Addresses • Addresses • Addresses • Addresses • Addresses • Addresses

C

Name

✉

☎

Name

✉

☎

Name

✉

☎

Name

✉

☎

Name

✉

☎

Name

✉

☎

Suffering

"A Wounded Deer – leaps highest."
Emily Dickinson

"We are healed of a suffering only by experiencing it to the full."
Marcel Proust

"Sadness flies on the wings of the morning and out of the heart of darkness comes the light."
Jean Giraudoux

Travel

"The less a tourist knows, the fewer mistakes he need make, for he will not expect himself to explain ignorance."
Henry Adams

"He who would travel happily must travel light."
Saint-Exupéry

"He that travels much knows much."
Thomas Fuller

Weddings

"An ideal wife is any woman who has an ideal husband."
Booth Tarkington

"A man's wife has more power over him than the state has."
Ralph Waldo Emerson

"Any married man should forget his mistakes – no use two people remembering the same thing."
Duane Dewel

"Only two things are necessary to keep one's wife happy. One is to let her think she is having her own way, and the other, to let her have it."
Lyndon B Johnson

"Marriage is popular because it combines the maximum of temptation with the maximum of opportunity."
Shelley

"One of the best hearing aids a man can have is an attentive wife."
Groucho Marx

EVERYDAY THOUGHTS
for everyday living

"Blessed be childhood, which brings down something of heaven into the midst of our rough earthliness."

Henri Frédéric Amiel

"An agreeable companion on a journey is as good as a carriage."

Publilius Syrus

"What value has compassion that does not take its object in its arms?"

Saint-Exupéry

"Worse than idle is compassion
If it ends in tears and sighs."

William Wordsworth

"Content makes poor men rich; discontent makes rich men poor."

Benjamin Franklin

Addresses • Addresses • Addresses • Addresses • Addresses • Addresses • Addresses

C

Name

Name

Name

Name

Name

Name

IN THE KITCHEN ~ WEIGHTS, MEASURES & TEMPERATURES

COOKING (DIAL MARKINGS)

Gasmark	¼	1	2	3	4
Fahrenheit	250	275	300	325	350
Celsius	120	140	150	160	180

Gasmark	5	6	7	8	9
Fahrenheit	375	400	425	450	475
Celsius	190	200	220	230	240

OVEN TEMPERATURES

Gasmark	Description
¼	Very Slow
½	Very Slow
1	Slow
2	Slow
3	Moderate
4	Moderate
5	Moderately Hot
6	Moderately Hot
7	Hot
8	Hot
9	Very Hot

Conversions given are approximate.
Never mix metric and imperial measures in one recipe - stick to one system or the other.

TEMPERATURE CONVERSION CHART

°F	°C
212B	100B
122	50
113	45
104	40
95	35
86	30
77	25
68	20
59	15
50	10
41	5
32	0
23	-5
14	-10
5	-15
-4	-20

DRY WEIGHT

Approximate gram conversion to nearest round figure	Recommended gram conversion to nearest 25g	Imperial ounce (oz)
28	25	1
57	50	2
85	75	3
113	100-125	4 (¼lb)
142	150	5
170	175	6
198	200	7
227	225	8 (½lb)
255	250	9
284	275	10
311	300	11
340	350	12 (¾lb)
368	375	13
396	400	14
425	425	15
453	450	16 (1lb)

LIQUID MEASURES

Approx. mililitre conversion to nearest round figure	Recommended mililitre equivalent	Imperial pint	Imperial fluid ounce (oz)
568	575-600	1	20
284	300	½	10
142	150	¼	5

EVERYDAY THOUGHTS
for everyday living

"It is always darkest just before the day dawneth."

Thomas Fuller

"To die completely, a person must not only forget but be forgotten, and he who is not forgotten is not dead."

Samuel Butler

"Oh, what a tangled web we weave
When first we practise to deceive."

Walter Scott: Marmion

"Despair exaggerates not only our misery but also our weakness."

Luc de Vauvenargues

"Despair of nothing. [Nil desperandum]."

Latin Proverb

Addresses • Addresses • Addresses • Addresses • Addresses • Addresses • Addresses

D

Name

✉

☎

Name

✉

☎

Name

✉

☎

Name

✉

☎

Name

✉

☎

Name

✉

☎

FOOD & HEALTH

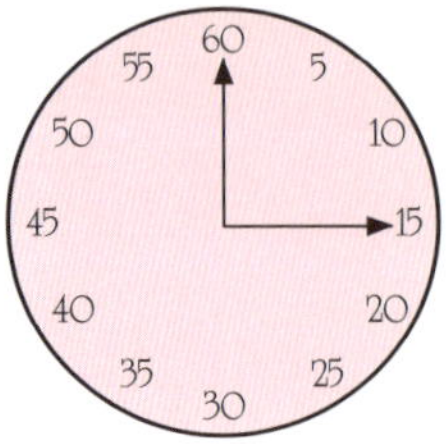

CALORIE EXPENDITURE

Below are given the approximate energy costs of some activities for a 70 kg adult:

Activity	Calories used per 15 min
Sitting	20
Sweeping	30
Sitting, writing	35
Sailing	40
Driving a car	48
Table tennis	50
Yoga	50
Walking slowly	55
Ironing	60
Cycling slowly	65
Surfing/wind surfing	65
Polishing the floor	68
Water skiing	70
Badminton	70
Golf	75
Walking fast	80
Ballet	80

Activity	Calories used per 15 min
Energetic dancing	85
Judo, karate, tai'chi	90
Skating, roller skating	90
Playing cricket - batting	100
Playing tennis	120
Jogging	120
Digging	130
Playing football	140
Shovelling earth	160
Cycling fast	168
Skiing downhill	175
Climbing with a pack	200
Running	200
Squash	230
Swimming fast	255
Skiing cross-country	280

EVERYDAY THOUGHTS
for everyday living

"Difficulties strengthen the mind,
as labour does the body."

Seneca

"The best way out of a difficulty
is through it."

Author Unidentified

"What we hope to do with ease, we
must first learn to do with diligence."

Samuel Johnson

"Our duty is to be useful,
not according to our desires,
but according to our powers."

Henri Frédérick Amiel

"The path of duty lies in the thing
that is nearby, but men seek it
in things far off."

Chinese Proverb

Addresses • Addresses • Addresses • Addresses • Addresses • Addresses • Addresses

D

Name

Name

Name

Name

Name

Name

FOOD & HEALTH ~ CALORIE COUNTING

Calories per ounce (25g) unless otherwise stated:

Anchovies	40
Apples	10
Apricots	
Canned in syrup	30
Dried	50
Fresh, with stone	5
Artichokes (boiled)	5
Asparagus	5
Aubergines	5
Sliced & fried (1oz raw)	60
Avocado Pears (flesh only)	65
Bacon	
Back raw	120
Streaky raw	115
Bananas (flesh only)	20
Bass (steamed fillet)	35
Bean Sprouts (raw)	10
Beans	
Baked beans	20
Broad (boiled)	15
Butter (boiled)	25
French (boiled)	neg
Haricot (boiled)	30
Kidney (canned)	25
Runner (boiled)	5
Soya (raw, dried)	115
Beef	
Brisket (boiled)	90
Minced beef (raw)	75
Minced beef (1oz raw, well fried & drained of fat)	45
Rump steak (fried, lean)	55
Rump steak (grilled, lean)	50
Sirloin (roast, lean & fat)	50
Stewing steak (raw)	50
Topside (roast, lean & fat)	60
Beetroot (boiled)	15
Blackberries (fresh)	10
Blackcurrants (fresh)	10
Black Pudding (raw)	105
Bran	60
Bread	
Brown/Wheatmeal/Hovis/White	65
Malt	70
Wholemeal	60
Bap (50g)	120
Croissant (50g)	270
Crusty roll	145
French Bread (50g)	130
Granary	70
Hot cross bun (50g)	180
Pitta bread (45g)	125
Rye bread	70
Tea cake (50g)	155
Broccoli (boiled)	5
Brussels Sprouts (boiled)	5
Butter	210
Cabbage (boiled)	5
Carrots (boiled)	5
Cauliflower (boiled)	5
Caviar	75
Celery	neg
Cheese	
Austrian Smoked	80
Babybel	95
Blue Stilton	130
Boursin	115
Brie	90
Cairphilly	120
Camembert	90
Cheddar	120
Cheshire	110
Cottage Cheese	25
Cream Cheese	125
Curd Cheese	40
Danish Blue	105
Danish Mozzarella	100
Double Gloucester	105
Edam	90
Emmenthal	115
Gorgonzola	110
Gouda (not matured)	95
Gruyere	130
Lancashire	110
Leicester	105
Norwegian Blue	100
Parmesan	115
Processed	90
Rambol (with walnuts)	115
Roquefort	90
Sage Derby	110
Wensleydale	115
White Stilton	95
Cherries	
Fresh with stones	10
Glace	60
Chicken	
On bone, raw	25
Meat only, raw	40
Meat & skin, roast	60
Chinese Leaves	neg
Chives	10
Chocolate	
Milk/Plain	150
Cooking	155
Cod	
On bone, raw	15
Fillet, raw	20
Fried in batter	55
Steamed fillet	25
Coffee (instant)	30
Corned Beef	60
Corn o/t Cob (boiled, kernels only)	35
Courgettes	5
Cream	
Clotted	165
Double	125
Single	60
Soured	55
Whipping	95
Cucumber	5
Currants	70
Dates (per date)	15
Duck	
Roast, meat only	55
Roast, meat, fat & skin	95

EVERYDAY THOUGHTS
for everyday living

"Early rising not only gives us more life in the same number of years, but adds, likewise, to their number."

Charles Cotton

"Education is what survives when what has been learnt has been forgotten."

B F Skinner

"Education is an ornament in prosperity and a refuge in adversity."

Aristotle

"Correction does much, but encouragement does more."

Johann Wolfgang von Goethe

"Love your enemies, bless them that curse you, do good to them that hate you, and pray for them which despitefully use you, and persecute you."

Matthew 5:44

Addresses • Addresses • Addresses • Addresses • Addresses • Addresses • Addresses

E

Name

✉

☎

Name

✉

☎

Name

✉

☎

Name

✉

☎

Name

✉

☎

Name

✉

☎

FOOD & HEALTH ~ CALORIE COUNTING

Eggs		
Graded Eggs	Raw	Fried
1	95	145
2	90	140
3	80	130
4	75	120
5	70	110
6	60	100
Yolk of size 3 egg		60
White of size 3 egg		15

Gherkins	5
Gooseberries (fresh, dessert)	10
Grapefruit	
Canned in syrup	15
Flesh only/With skin	5
Juice	10
Grapes	15
Haddock	
On bone, raw	15
Fillet, raw	20
On bone, smoked	20
Smoked fillet	30
Fried fillet in breadcrumbs	50
Hake	
On bone, raw	10
Fillet, raw	20
Fillet, steamed	30
Fillet, fried	60
Halibut	
On bone, steamed	30
Fillet, steamed	35
Ham	
Lean, boiled	60
Fatty, boiled	120
Herring	
On bone, grilled	40
Fillet, grilled	55
Honey	80
Ice-cream	45
Jam	75
Kidney (raw)	25
Kippers (baked or grilled fillet)	60
Lamb	
Roast breast, boned,	115
Roast breast, boned, lean only	75
Roast leg, boned,	75
Roast leg, boned, lean only	55
Roast shoulder, lean & fat	90
Roast shoulder, lean only	55
Leeks (raw)	10
Lemon Sole	
On bone (grilled or steamed)	20
Fillet (grilled or steamed)	25
Lentils (boiled)	30
Lettuce (raw)	5
Liver	
Chicken's, fried	55
Lamb's, fried	65
Ox, stewed	55
Pig's, stewed	55
Liver sausage	90
Lobster	
With shell, boiled	10
Meat only, boiled	35
Macaroni (boiled)	35
Mackerel	
On bone, fried	40
Fillet, fried	55
Smoked	70
Mandarins	
Canned	15
Fresh, with skin	5
Margarine	205
Marmalade	75
Marzipan	125
Mayonnaise	205
Melon (with skin)	5
Milk	
Gold Top	430
Red Top	370
Longlife/UHT	370
Low-fat powdered	200
Pasteurised/SIlver Top	370
Skimmed	200
Sterilized	370
Evaporated	45
Condensed (sweetened)	90
Muesli	105
Mushrooms (raw)	5
Mussels	
Boiled, with shells	5
Boiled, without shells	25
Nectarines	15
Noodles (cooked)	35
Nuts (mixed, roasted, salted)	175
Olive Oil	255
Olives (with stones, in brine)	25
Onions	
Raw	5
Fried	100
Rings fried in batter	145
Oranges	
Flesh only	10
With skin	5
Juice	10
Parsnips (raw or boiled)	15
Peaches	
Fresh, with stones	10
Canned in syrup	25
Peanuts	
Shelled or roasted, salted	160
Peanut butter	175
Pears	
Fresh	10
Canned in syrup	20
Peas	
Fresh, raw	20
Fresh, boiled	15
Canned, garden	15

Canned, processed	25
Chick, raw	90
Perch	
White	35
Yellow	25
Pheasant	
Roast, on bone	40
Roast, meat only	60
Pilchards (canned in tomato sauce)	35

EVERYDAY THOUGHTS
for everyday living

"Let age, not envy, draw wrinkles
on thy cheeks."

Sir Thomas Browne

"The quality of a person's life is in
direct proportion to their commitment
to excellence, regardless of their
chosen field of endeavour."

Vince Lombardi

"He that is good for making excuses
is seldom good for anything else."

Benjamin Franklin

"Experience is not what happens
to you; it is what you do with
what happens to you."

Aldous Huxley

"To most men, experience is like the
stern lights of a ship, which illumine
only the track it has passed."

S T Coleridge

Addresses • Addresses • Addresses • Addresses • Addresses • Addresses • Addresses • Addresses

E

Name

Name

Name

Name

Name

Name

FOOD & HEALTH ~ CALORIE COUNTING

Pineapples	
Fresh	15
Canned in syrup	20
Plaice (fillet)	
Raw or steamed	25
Fried in batter	80
Fried in crumbs	65
Plums	
Fresh dessert, with stones	10
Cooking, with stones	5
Pork	
Roast, lean & fat	80
Roast, lean meat only	50
Cracking	190
Scratchings	185
Prawns	
With shells	10
Without shells	30

Prunes	
Dried	45
Stewed (no sugar)	25
Rabbit	
On bone, stewed	25
Meat only, stewed	50
Radishes	5
Raspberries	
Fresh	5
Tinned, drained	25
Redcurrants (fresh)	5
Rhubarb	neg
Rice	
Raw	100
Boiled	35
Salmon	
Raw, on bone	50
Steamed, on bone	45
Steamed, fillet	55
Canned	45
Smoked	40
Sardines	
Canned in oil, drained	60
Canned in tomato sauce	50
Sausages	
Pork, lightly fried or grilled	165
Pork, well fried or grilled	115
Pork, chipolata:	
lightly fried or grilled	165
well fried or grilled	115
Beef, fried or grilled	120
Beef, chipolata fried or grilled	120
Scampi (fried in breadcrumbs)	90
Semolina (raw)	100
Shrimps	
With shells	10
Without shells	35
Canned	25
Skate (fillet fried in batter)	55
Sole	
Fillet, raw	25
Fillet, fried	60
Fillet, steamed	25
On bone, steamed	20
Spaghetti	
Raw	105
Boiled	35
Canned in tomato sauce	15
Spinach (boiled)	10
Spring Onions	10
Strawberries	
Fresh	5
Tinned, drained	25
Sturgeon (on bone, raw)	25
Sugar	110
Sultanas (dried)	70
Sunflower Seed Oil	255
Swedes	5
Sweetcorn	
Canned	20
Fresh boiled, kernels	35
Frozen	25
Sweets	
Boiled sweets	95
Filled chocolates	130
Fudge	110
Peppermints	110
Toffee	120
Syrup	
Golden	85
Maple	70
Tangerines	
Flesh only	10
With skin	5
Tapioca (dry)	100
Tea	neg
Tomatoes	
Canned	5
Fried, halved	20
Fried, sliced	30
Ketchup	30
Puree	20
Raw	5
Tongue (Ox, boiled)	85
Treacle (Black)	85
Tripe (Stewed)	30
Trout	
Fillet, smoked	35
On bone, steamed	25
Tuna	
Canned in oil	80
Drained of oil	60
Turkey	
Meat only, roast	40
Meat & skin, roast	50
Turnips (raw)	5
Veal	
Escalope, fried (egg/b'crumbs)	60
Fillet, raw	30
Fillet, roast	65
Venison (roast, meat)	55
Watermelon	5
Whitebait (fried)	150
Whiting	
On bone, fried	50
Fillet, fried	55
On bone, steamed	20
Fillet, steamed	25
Yorkshire Pudding (cooked)	60

'neg' signifies negligible calorie content

EVERYDAY THOUGHTS
for everyday living

"If your life is free of failures,
you're not taking enough risks."

Author Unidentified

"There is no failure except in
no longer trying."

Elbert Hubbard

"Only the person who has faith in
himself is able to be faithful to others."

Erich Fromm

"The greatest of faults is to be
conscious of none."

Thomas Carlyle

"Present fears are less than
horrible imaginings."

Shakespeare: Macbeth

Addresses • Addresses • Addresses • Addresses • Addresses • Addresses • Addresses • Addresses

F

Name

✉

☎

Name

✉

☎

Name

✉

☎

Name

✉

☎

Name

✉

☎

Name

✉

☎

Cooking Times & Methods of Some Vegetables

Vegetable	Steam	Boil	Bake (Whole)	Braise	Stir Fry
Asparagus		10-15 mins			
Beetroot		40-60 mins			
Broad Beans		10-15 mins			
Broccoli	4-8 mins				yes
Brussels Sprouts	6-10 mins		25-30 mins		yes
Cabbage	4-6 mins				yes
Carrots	20 mins	10-15 mins	45-60 mins	15-20 mins	yes
Cauliflower	4-8 mins				
Celery	12-15 mins	8-10 mins		10-12 mins	yes
Chicory					yes
Chinese Leaves	4 mins				yes
Courgettes	4-8 mins				yes
Cucumbers	5-10 mins				
Endive				10-12 mins	
Fennel	12-15 mins	10-12 mins		15-20 mins	yes
French Beans	4-8 mins				yes
Globe Artichokes		30-40 mins			
Jerusalem Artichokes		15-20 mins			
Leeks	15-20 mins	10-15 mins		8-10 mins	
Mangetout Peas	6-8 mins				yes
Marrow	10-12 mins		45-60 mins		yes
Mushrooms					yes
Okra		15-20 mins			
Onions			45-60 mins		
Parsnips		15-20 mins	45-60 mins	15-20 mins	
Peas		8-12 mins			yes
Peppers					yes
Potatoes	25-30 mins	20 mins	1-1½ hours	15-20 mins	
Radish/Daikon					yes
Red Cabbage				45-60 mins	
Swedes	25-30 mins	20 mins		15-20 mins	yes
Sweet Potato	25-30 mins	20 mins	1-1½ hours		
Sweetcorn		8-15 mins			yes
Turnips	25-30 mins	10-15 mins		15-20 mins	yes

These are suggestions only and will give very lightly cooked vegetables. Increase the cooking time for softer vegetables.
The freshness of the vegetables may also affect the cooking time.

EVERYDAY THOUGHTS
for everyday living

"The only thing we have to fear
is fear itself."

F D Roosevelt

"Forgiveness is the answer to the child's dream of a miracle by which what is broken is made whole again, what is soiled is again made clean."

Dag Hammarskjold

"I keep my friends as misers do their treasure, because, of all the things granted us by wisdom, none is greater or better than friendship."

Pietro Aretino

"A true friend is the greatest of all blessings."

François de la Rochefoucauld

"I like the dreams of the future better than the history of the past."

Thomas Jefferson

Addresses • Addresses • Addresses • Addresses • Addresses • Addresses • Addresses

F

Name

Name

Name

Name

Name

Name

IN THE KITCHEN ~ HERBS & SPICES

HERBS

Herbs play an essential role in any kitchen, adding flavour and distinction to many dishes. All are available fresh or dried but remember that fresh herbs have a milder flavour and use roughly 15ml (1 tablespoon) of fresh herbs to 5ml (1 teaspoon) of dried.

Basil (Ocimum basilicum)

Two types of basil are grown; sweet and bush. The one most commonly found is sweet basil, which has largish, shiny, green leaves and a strong but sweet flavour. It is one of the best herbs to add to tomatoes, eggs, mushrooms and pasta dishes, forms part of a classic bouquet garni, and is an essential part of pesto sauce. Basil does not dry very successfully.

Bay Leaves (Laurus nobilis)

Sweet bay or bay laurel is a Mediterranean tree. The leaves are shiny, smooth and dark with a strong aromatic scent. It is often added to stocks when poaching fish, or to marinades, casseroles, soups and stews. It can also be used to flavour milk puddings.

Chervil (Anthriscus cerefolium)

Chervil is a member of the parsley family and is very popular with French chefs. It has a delicate fern-like leaf, offering a delicate taste with a hint of anise. It is especially good in soups, egg and cheese dishes, or added for flavour to green salad. It can also be used as a garnishing leaf.

Chives (Allium schoenoprasum)

A member of the onion family, chives have a mild onion flavour and long, spiky, green leaves. Raw chives are frequently used in salads, but can be added to omelettes, cheese dishes, and, mixed with soured cream, used as a topping for baked potatoes.

Coriander (Coriandrum sativum)

Coriander has flat feathery leaves and is often confused with flat parsley. It has a distinctive spicy flavour and is popular in Southern European, Indian and South East Asian cooking. The leaves are chopped and added to curries, stews, soups and marinades. It is also known as Chinese or Japanese parsley, and is used in the same way as parsley.

Dill (Anethum graveolens)

A delicate, feathery herb with an aromatic, sharp but sweet flavour. One of the most popular herbs in Scandinavia, it is especially good with fish if added to the marinade, cooking liquid or accompanying sauces. It can also be added to vegetables, cream or cottage cheese.

Lemon Balm (Melissa officinalis)

The crushed leaves of this plant, as the name would suggest, give off a wonderful lemony scent, making them ideal for use in salads.

Marjoram (Origanum majorana)

Sweet marjoram, a plant native to the Mediterranean, has small, furry leaves and a flavour similar to oregano but sweeter and milder. It can be added to most savoury dishes and is good with marrow, potatoes and rice. It is very fragrant and can be dried successfully.

EVERYDAY THOUGHTS
for everyday living

"Generosity gives assitance
rather than advice."

Luc de Vauvenargues

"Genius is 1 per cent inspiration
and 99 per cent perspiration."

Thomas A Edison

"Nothing is so strong as gentleness,
and nothing is so gentle as
real strength."

Ralph W Sockman

"The great mind knows the
power of gentleness,
Only tries force because
persuasion fails."

Robert Browning

"Grace is the absence of everything
that indicates pain or difficulty,
hesitation or incongruity."

William Hazlitt

G

Name

Name

Name

Name

Name

Name

IN THE KITCHEN ~ HERBS & SPICES

Mint (Menta spp.)
There are many species of this popular herb, from spearmint to the fresh-tasting peppermint used for tisanes. It is probably the best known herb in Britain and most commonly used with lamb and new potatoes. It can also be added to other young vegetables or chopped with minced beef, or mixed with yogurt for a dip. It also combines well with fruit.

Oregano (Origanum vulgare)
Oregano is wild marjoram, and, as it has the best flavour when grown in strong sun, is popular in Mediterranean cuisines - especially those of Italy and Greece. The flavour is similar to marjoram but stronger and the leaves are larger and darker. It enhances many meat dishes and it is often added to salads, pizza and tomato based dishes. Oregano can be dried successfully, keeping all its aroma.

Parsley (Petroselinum crispum)
There are two types of parsley: curled and flat. Flat (or French) parsley is generally grown in Europe and is considered to have a finer taste than curled parsley, but both are strong in Vitamin C and iron. Parsley is an essential part of a bouquet garni. It enlivens most savoury dishes and is often simply used as a garnish, either chopped or as sprigs. The chopped leaves can be added to salads, soups, sauces and cooked vegetables. It is said that if chewed after eating garlic it will remove the smell.

Rosemary (Rosmarinus officinalis)
A pungent, fragrant shrub with small, narrow leaves, set densely on the branches. It is often used with lamb but can be used with other meats and in vegetable dishes such as ratatouille or added to marinades.

Sage (Salvia officinalis)
Sage comes in many varieties and is a strongly flavoured herb with narrow, pale grey-green leaves with a rough texture. It has traditionally been used with pork, liver, and in stuffing, but can be used with any richly flavoured meat, and in cheese and tomato dishes. It dries well but can become musty if kept too long.

Savory (Satureja)
There are two varieties of savory: Winter savory (Satureja montana), and Summer savory (Satureja hortensis). The German name for winter savory means "bean-herb", indicating its traditional use, while summer savory is similar and even more aromatic.

Tarragon (Artemisia dracunculus)
There are two varieties of this herb: French and Russian. The French variety is harder to grow but is far more aromatic than the Russian. It has a distinctive flavour and shiny narrow leaves. It is widely used in vinegars, soups, stuffings, sauces, and salad dressings, and is also good with roast meat, poultry dishes and fish.

Thyme (Thymus vulgaris)
This popular herb contains an essential oil, thymol, which helps to digest fatty foods. Its small, dark-green bushy leaves have a very strong flavour. It is another herb which should be used in a bouquet garni, and it can be used to flavour meat, fish, soups, stews and vegetables.

EVERYDAY THOUGHTS
for everyday living

"Gratitude is the heart's memory."

French Proverb

"No metaphysician ever felt
the deficiency of language so much
as the grateful."

C C Colton

"A grateful mind, by owing owes not,
but still pays, at once
Indebted and discharged."

Milton: Paradise Lost

"Gratefulness is
the poor man's payment."

English Proverb

"The only cure for grief is action."

G H Lewes

"Nothing speaks our grief so well
As to speak nothing."

Richard Crashaw

G

Name

✉

☎

Name

✉

☎

Name

✉

☎

Name

✉

☎

Name

✉

☎

Name

✉

☎

IN THE KITCHEN ~ HERBS & SPICES

SPICES

Spices are the dried parts of aromatic plants and may be the fruit, root, flower, bud, bark or seed. For the best flavour, grind your own spices just before use.

Aniseed (Pimpinella asinum)
Aniseed has a strong liquorice flavour and is popular in Mexico and all over the Mediterranean.

Capers (Capparis spinosa)
The buds of a small Mediterranean bush, these are usually sold pickled in vinegar and should not be allowed to dry out. While they are used mostly in sauces and salads, they are also popular as a pizza topping, adding an authentic Mediterranean flavour.

Caraway (Carum carvi)
Caraway is in appearance similar to cumin seed and because of this is often confused with it. The taste, however, is very different.

Cardamom (Elettaria cardamomum)
Cardamom is a relative of the ginger family, available both whole green, black or white or ground. The most common is the grey-green pod which contains minute, dark brown seeds with an unmistakable bitter-sweet flavour with a hint of lemon and eucalyptus. It is used extensively in sweet and savoury Indian cookery as well as in Europe and the Middle East for cakes, biscuits and pickles and to flavour drinks.

Chili (Capsicum frutescens)
Ripe chili peppers dry and keep well and are most commonly used in chili powder, a very hot spice, whose blend may vary due to the numerous varieties of chilies to be found. Cayenne is a very hot, pungent red chili sold ready ground. Milder chili powders can be found or you can use chili seasoning which is a blend of ground dried chilis with other spices. It is used (sparingly) in meat, fish, poultry and egg dishes as well as soups, sauces and pickles.

Cinnamon (Cinnamomum zeylanicum)
The distinctive sticks of dried bark are harvested from the young shoots of a large, tropical evergreen. While it is best purchased as sticks and used whole or ground, is also available as a powder and has a sweet pungent flavour. Cinnamon is usually added to savoury dishes in the East and to sweet dishes in the West, and is used in apple desserts, cakes and mulled drinks.

Cloves (Eugenia caryophyllata)
Cloves are the unopened flower buds of the tropical evergreen clove tree. They become rich brown in colour when dried and resemble small nails in shape. Cloves have a penetrating taste and are available whole or ground: if used whole then they are best removed before a dish is eaten. They are used mainly to flavour fruit dishes, mulled wine, mincemeat, bread sauce and curries.

Coriander (Coriandrum sativum)
Coriander is a member of the parsley family. The aromatic brown seeds have a sweet orangey flavour. Sold whole or ground, they are quite mild so can be used more freely than most spices and are used widely in Arab and Eastern cookery; in curries, casseroles, soups, dishes such as couscous and hummus and with vegetables and chutneys.

EVERYDAY THOUGHTS
for everyday living

"We first make our habits,
and then our habits make us."

Author Unidentified

"Success is getting what you
want. Happiness is liking
what you get."

Author Unidentified

"Happiness makes up in height
for what it lacks in length."

Robert Frost

"We have no more right to consume
happiness without producing it
than to consume wealth without
producing it."

George Bernard Shaw

"When I was at home, I was in
a better place."

Shakespeare: As You Like It

Addresses • Addresses • Addresses • Addresses • Addresses • Addresses • Addresses

H

Name

✉

☎

Name

✉

☎

Name

✉

☎

Name

✉

☎

Name

✉

☎

Name

✉

☎

IN THE KITCHEN ~ HERBS & SPICES

Cumin (Cuminum cyminum)

Cumin is a member of the parsley family and is available both as seeds or in powdered form. It has a sharp, spicy, slightly bitter taste and should be used in moderation. It is often combined with coriander as a basic curry mixture, but is also used for flavouring Middle Eastern fish recipes, casseroles and couscous. It can be added to pickles, chutneys, soups and rice dishes.

Ginger (Zingiber officinale)

Ginger is a distinctive knobbly root with a hot sweetish taste sold in several forms. Fresh root ginger, essential for many Eastern recipes, releases its true flavour on cooking. It is peeled and then sliced or grated for use in curries, Chinese cooking or marinades for meat, fish and poultry. Dried ginger is the dried ground root and is best used in preserves, cakes, biscuits and puddings. Stem ginger is available preserved in syrup or crystallized and is a sweetmeat either eaten whole, with carel, or used in breads, cakes, confectionery and desserts.

Juniper (Juniperus communis)

Juniper berries have a pungent, slightly resinous flavour. They go well with cabbage and add a light touch to oily or heavy dishes.

Mace (Myristica fragrans)

Mace is the dried outer membrane of nutmeg. It is sold both as blades or ground, although ground mace quickly loses its flavour. It is used in mulled wines and punches, meat pies, loaves, stews, savoury white sauces and in milk puddings.

Nutmeg (Myristica fragrans)

Nutmeg has a brown uneven outer surface with a pale interior, is milder than mace although slightly nuttier and is available whole or ground, but as it loses its flavour quickly, is best grated as required. It can be sprinkled on vegetables and is used in soups, sauces, meat terrines, pates, and puddings.

Paprika (Capsicum annum)

A finely ground red powder made from the fruits of several chili plants, popular in Hungary and Spain. The flesh only is used for mild sweet paprikas whilst the seeds are included in more pungent paprikas. Use to add colour to egg and cheese dishes, in salads, with fish and shellfish, chicken and classically in Hungarian Goulash.

Saffron (Crocus sativus)

Saffron is the dried stigmas of the saffron crocus flower. It is very expensive, as it is individually handpicked and imparts a slightly bitter honey-like flavour and a yellow colour. It is safer to buy the threads as the powder is easy to adulterate. It is added to rice dishes, Spanish Paella, Bouillabaisse and to Cornish Saffron cake.

Turmeric (Circuma longa)

Turmeric is the dried root of a plant from the ginger family, usually sold ground, although sometimes sold fresh. It has a strong woody aroma and a slightly bitter flavour and is used to colour rice, pickles, cakes and in curries and dhals. It is sometimes used as a cheap substitute for saffron to colour dishes, but the flavour is not the same.

Vanilla (Vanilla planifolia)

Vanilla is the fruit of an orchid plant found in Mexico. It has traditionally been used to flavour chocolate, and is good in many sweet dishes, though it is expensive to buy.

EVERYDAY THOUGHTS
for everyday living

"We should not let our fears hold us back from pursuing our hopes."

John F Kennedy

"The hope set before us . . . is like an anchor for our lives, an anchor safe and sure."

Hebrews 6.19

"When there is room in the heart there is room in the house."

Danish Proverb

"Hospitality is to be shown even towards an enemy. The tree doth not withdraw its shade, even from the woodcutter."

The Hitopadesa

"Better is it to be of a humble spirit with the lowly than to divide the spoil with the proud."

Proverbs 16:19

Addresses • Addresses • Addresses • Addresses • Addresses • Addresses • Addresses

H

Name

✉

☎

Name

✉

☎

Name

✉

☎

Name

✉

☎

Name

✉

☎

Name

✉

☎

FROM TURKEY

CACIK

Ingredients

1 cucumber
3/4 pint yogurt
salt, white pepper
2-3 cloves garlic
3 tbsp chopped mint

Method

Peel & dice cucumber, then sprinkle with salt and leave in colander for half an hour. Crush garlic with a little salt, add to yogurt and mix well. Add salt, pepper and mint, drain cucumber and stir in. Garnish with mint.

IMAM BAYILDI

Ingredients

3 large onions
olive oil
12 oz tomatoes
1/2 tsp cinnamon
1 tsp castor sugar
3 large aubergines (with leaf bases cut off)
1 clove garlic
1 tbsp chopped parsley
1 heaped tbsp finely chopped pine kernels (optional)
salt, black pepper

Method

Wipe the aubergines and put in large saucepan. Add boiling water and cover. Cook for 10 mins, drain, then plunge into cold water. Leave for 5 mins, cut in half lengthways, scoop out most of flesh, leaving half-inch thick shells. Arrange shells in buttered overproof dish and sprinkle with salt and pepper. Pour 4 tbsp olive oil into each shell and cook, uncovered, in pre-heated oven (350°F or equivalent) for 30 mins. While aubergines are cooking, peel and finely chop onions, skin and chop tomatoes and crush garlic. Heat 2 tbsp of oil in a frying pan, add onions and garlic and fry gently for 5 mins, then add tomatoes, cinnamon, sugar and parsley; season to taste. Simmer until liquid has reduced by half (about 20 mins). Chop aubergine flesh and add to frying pan with pine kernels and cook for 10 mins. Remove aubergine shells from oven, stuff with tomato mixture and serve hot or cold.

TURKISH YOGURT

Ingredients

2 cartons natural yogurt
1 tsp castor sugar
2 oz seedless raisins
1 tbsp lemon juice
1 tsp lemon rind
1 tbsp desiccated coconut

Method

Mix all ingredients together, put in covered dish and chill. Leave to stand for at least one hour before serving to allow flavour to develop.

EVERYDAY THOUGHTS
for everyday living

"Man's mind once stretched by a new idea, never regains its original dimension."

Oliver Wendell Holmes

"Idleness, like kisses, to be sweet must be stolen."

Jerome K Jerome

"There is always hope in a man who actually and earnestly works. In idleness alone is there perpetual despair."

Thomas Carlyle

"The man with imagination is never alone."

Author Unidentified

"By asking for the impossible we obtain the best possible."

Italian Proverb

Addresses • Addresses • Addresses • Addresses • Addresses • Addresses • Addresses

J

Name

✉

☎

Name

✉

☎

Name

✉

☎

Name

✉

☎

Name

✉

☎

Name

✉

☎

IN THE KITCHEN ~ INTERNATIONAL RECIPES

FROM GREECE

TARAMASALATA

Ingredients

- 8 oz smoked cod roe (fresh or tinned)
- 6-8 tbsp olive oil
- juice of 1 large lemon
- black pepper

Method

Place roe in a mixing bowl. Add oil and lemon juice alternately, a little at a time, and beat vigorously after each addition until the mixture is a creamy paté. Season to taste with freshly ground black pepper and pack into a dish. Cover and chill lightly. Serve with hot crisp toast, unsalted butter, black olives and lemon wedges.

DOLMADES

Ingredients

- 12 fresh vine/cabbage leaves or a 7 oz tin of vine leaves
- 1 lb lean lamb, minced
- 1 onion
- 4 oz long grain rice
- 3 oz butter
- 1 1/2 pints of white stock
- 1 dsp chopped fresh mint or parsley
- 1 tsp powdered rosemary
- salt, black pepper
- juice of half a lemon
- 5 fl oz yogurt

Method

Peel onion and chop finely. Melt 1 oz butter and fry onion and rice until lightly coloured. Add enough stock to cover rice and cook over low heat until tender, stirring frequently. Leave to cool. Stir in minced lamb, herbs and salt and pepper. Blanch the fresh vine or cabbage leaves for a few minutes in boiling water, spread out and put a spoonful of lamb and rice filling on each; fold the leaves over to make small, neat parcels. Pack carefully in layers in casserole pan. Put a plate on top to keep the parcels under the liquid. Cover and simmer for one hour. Serve yogurt separately.

HISTORIAN'S PUDDING

Ingredients

- 2 oz self-raising flour
- 4 oz fresh breadcrumbs
- 4 oz suet
- 8 oz raisins
- 1 tbsp allspice
- 1 tbsp milk
- 1 oz sugar
- 2 chopped dried figs
- grated rind of 1/2 lemon
- 2 eggs, beaten
- 2 tbsp sherry

Method

Mix all dry ingredients together. Stir in eggs and sherry, then add milk to make a soft dough. Put in buttered pudding basin and cover with foil. Steam for 3-4 hours and serve hot with sherry sauce.

EVERYDAY THOUGHTS
for everyday living

"Nature knows no pause in her progress and development, and attaches her curse on all inaction."

Johann Wolfgang von Goethe

"He's armed without that's innocent within."

Alexander Pope

"A man is not to aim at innocence any more than he is to aim at hair, but he is to keep it."

Ralph Waldo Emerson

"A moment's insight is sometimes worth a life's experience."

Oliver Wendell Holmes

"Instinct is intelligence incapable of selfconciousness."

John Sterling

Name

✉

☎

Name

✉

☎

Name

✉

☎

Name

✉

☎

Name

✉

☎

Name

✉

☎

IN THE KITCHEN ~ INTERNATIONAL RECIPES

FROM AMERICA

TUNA WALDORF SALAD

Ingredients

- 2 7-oz tins of tuna
- 1 cup diced apples
- 1/2 cup chopped celery
- crumbled blue cheese
- 1/4 cup walnuts
- 1/2 cup mayonnaise
- lettuce

Method

Drain and flake the tuna. In a bowl combine all ingredients except lettuce and blue cheese. Mix well. Serve on lettuce leaves. Garnish with crumbled blue cheese.

SLOPPY JOES

Ingredients

- 1 lb minced beef
- 1 large onion
- 1 green pepper
- 2 tbsp American mustard
- 1 tsp brown sugar
- 2 tsp cloves
- 2 tsp white sugar
- 2 tsp vinegar
- tomato ketchup
- 10 bread rolls

Method

Chop the onion and the green pepper and fry the meat until it is brown. Then add the rest of the ingredients. Mix together and fry for about 10 minutes. 'Slop' onto hamburger style buns.

PUMPKIN PIE

Ingredients

For the Pastry:

- 6 oz plain flour
- 3 oz butter
- milk or water
- pinch of salt
- 4 oz soft brown sugar
- 1 tsp cinnamon
- 1 tsp mace
- 1/4 tsp ground nutmeg

For the Filling:

- 1 14-oz tin pumpkin (or fresh pumpkin)
- 1/4 pint milk
- 2 eggs, lightly beaten
- 1 1/2 tsp salt
- 1/4 pint single cream

Method

Preheat oven to 450°F. Prepare blind pastry shell but do not bake it. Combine all the filling ingredients, mixing well. Pour into the pie crust. Bake in oven for 15 mins, then lower temperature to 350°F and bake till firm - about another 50 mins. Serve warm or cold with grated cheese on top or with cream.

EVERYDAY THOUGHTS
for everyday living

"Though jealousy be produced by love, as ashes are by fire, yet jealousy extinguishes love as ashes smother the flame."

Margaret of Navarre

"It is not love that is blind, but jealousy."

Lawrence Durrell

"Jealousy: that dragon which slays love under the pretense of keeping it alive."

Havelock Ellis

"A wise man sings his joy in the closet of his heart."

Tibullus

"All who joy would win
Must share it, -
Happiness was born a Twin."

Byron: Don Juan

Name

✉

☎

Name

✉

☎

Name

✉

☎

Name

✉

☎

Name

✉

☎

Name

✉

☎

FROM FRANCE

FRENCH ONION SOUP

Ingredients

- 2 oz butter or margarine
- 2 large onions
- 2 pints of stock
- sliced French bread
- grated Gruyère cheese
- seasoning

Method

Slice onion thinly and fry in butter, add the stock and simmer for about 30 minutes. Season with salt and pepper. Meanwhile, sprinkle cheese on bread slices and brown under a hot grill. Put bread in bottom of soup bowls and pour soup on top.

QUICHE LORRAINE

Ingredients

- 8 oz shortcrust pastry
- 1 onion
- 4 rashers bacon
- 1 small leek, chopped
- 1/4 pint milk
- 3 eggs
- 2 oz grated cheese
- seasoning

Method

Make pastry and with it line a deep 7-inch sandwich tin, or a flan ring or a 1 pint deep ovenproof plate. Chop the onion and bacon into small pieces and then fry in margarine until tender. Turn them into the pastry case. Beat eggs, stir in the milk, seasoning and most of the cheese, and add the chopped leek. Pour this mixture into the case, sprinkle rest of cheese on top. Bake the flan until it is just set and golden brown on top, 350°F or Gas Mark 5 for 35-40 minutes.

FRENCH CUSTARD ICE CREAM

Ingredients

- 2 large eggs
- 1/2 pint single cream
- 3 tbsp granulated sugar
- 2 tsp vanilla essence

Method

Set fridge to its coldest setting one hour before making ice cream. Place cream, eggs and sugar into a double saucepan with water simmering. Sitr continuously until the custard is thick enough to coat thinly the back of a spoon. Do not let it boil. Pour into a bowl, stir in the vanilla essence and cool. Pour when cold into ice cube tray and place in the freezer section of your fridge. Freeze until ice cream has frozen about 1/2 inch round sides of tray (about 1 hour). Turn into chilled bowl and whisk until smooth. Return to washed and dried tray and freeze until firm (a further 1 1/2 to 2 hours).

EVERYDAY THOUGHTS
for everyday living

"He who binds to himself a joy
Does the winged life destroy;
But he who kisses the joy as it flies
Lives in eternity's sunrise."

William Blake

"Joy is for all men. It does not depend on circumstance or condition: if it did, it could only be for the few."

Horace Bushnell

"If you judge, investigate."
[Si judicas, cognosce.]

Seneca

"He hath a good judgement that relieth not wholly on his own."

Thomas Fuller

"Extreme justice is often unjust."

Racine

Addresses • Addresses • Addresses • Addresses • Addresses • Addresses • Addresses

J

Name

Name

Name

Name

Name

Name

IN THE KITCHEN ~ INTERNATIONAL RECIPES

FROM JAPAN

NABEMONO (COD SOUP)

Ingredients

- 2 fillets cod
- 3 leeks
- Chinese leaves or spinach
- 12 mushrooms
- 2 packets bean cake (available from health food shops)
- soy sauce

Method

Cut cod into small pieces and cut bean cake into cubes. Wash vegetables and put water in large saucepan. When hot but not boiling, add fish and bean cake. Bring to boil and skim off froth. Add all the vegetables. Simmer for 10 minutes.

TAKIKOMI GOHAN (CHICKEN RICE)

Ingredients

- 4 cups pudding rice
- 3 tbsp saki or white wine
- soy sauce
- 1 pinch salt
- 1 carrot
- 3 mushrooms
- $^1/_4$ chicken
- $^1/_2$ lb french beans

Method

Wash rice until the water is clear and leave to drain for 30 minutes. Slice carrot and mushrooms and cut chicken into very small pieces. Put about 4 $^1/_2$ cups of water in saucepan, add rice and all ingredients except the beans. Bring to boil on high heat then remove lid. Leave boiling hard for 2 minutes. When water is almost gone and air holes appear in rice, turn heat down very low. Meanwhile boil french beans very lightly in salted water. Chop up with butter and mix with rice before serving.

YAKITOR (CHICKEN)

Ingredients

- 4 chicken pieces
- soy sauce
- saki or white wine
- ground ginger
- 1 red chili
- 1 garlic clove

Method

Chop chili and garlic and wash chicken. Put all ingredients in dish and leave overnight, turning occasionally. Before the meal, grill the chicken.

This can be served with raw vegetables or salad, cucumber, tomatoes, chopped cabbage, grated carrots, lettuce etc.

EVERYDAY THOUGHTS
for everyday living

"You can accomplish by kindness what you cannot do by force."

Publilius Syrus

"One who knows how to show and to accept kindness will be a friend better than any possession."

Sophocles

"I expect to pass through life but once. If, therefore, there be any kindness I can show, or any good thing I can do for any fellow being, let me do it now, for I shall not pass this way again."

William Penn

"The smallest act of kindness is worth more than the grandest intention."

Author Unidentified

Addresses • Addresses • Addresses • Addresses • Addresses • Addresses • Addresses

K

Name

✉

☎

Name

✉

☎

Name

✉

☎

Name

✉

☎

Name

✉

☎

Name

✉

☎

IN THE KITCHEN ~ INTERNATIONAL RECIPES

FROM ITALY

SPAGHETTI BOLOGNESE

Ingredients

- 1 onion
- 1 $^{1}/_{2}$ oz butter
- 1 dsp olive oil
- $^{1}/_{2}$ lb minced beef
- $^{1}/_{2}$ pint water
- 4 oz cheddar cheese
- 1 garlic clove
- $^{1}/_{4}$ lb mushrooms
- 5oz tin tomato purée
- 2 tsp sugar
- $^{1}/_{2}$ tsp mixed herbs
- $^{3}/_{4}$ lb spaghetti
- seasoning
- Bay leaf

Method

Chop onion and fry gently, add meat and fry for 4 minutes, stirring. Add chopped garlic and sliced mushrooms together with water, sugar, bay leaf, tomato purée, herbs and seasoning. Bring to boil and simmer for 30 minutes, stirring often. Boil spaghetti for 20 minutes in salted water. Drain and serve with sauce and finely grated cheese.

RISOTTO MILANESE

Ingredients

- 1 small onion
- 3 oz butter
- 1 $^{1}/_{2}$ pints chicken stock
- $^{3}/_{4}$ lb long grain rice
- 3 oz cheese
- seasoning

Method

Fry chopped onion gently in 2 oz butter. Add rice and fry for 1 minute, stirring Gradually add hot stock. Simmer in covered pan for 25 minutes, stirring often. Add 1 oz butter and 1 oz cheese. Serve with grated cheese.

MILANESE SOUFFLE

Ingredients

- 2 lemons
- 3 eggs, separated
- 4 oz sugar
- $^{1}/_{2}$ pint double cream
- $^{1}/_{2}$ oz gelatine
- 5 tbsp water
- chopped nuts, whipped cream, glacé cherries & angelica (for decoration)

Method

Dissolve gelatine in water, using bowl in saucepan of warm water. To another bowl in warm water add egg yolks, sugar, juice and grated rinds from lemons, whisking until thick and creamy. Remove from heat and whisk until the outside of the bowl is cold. Fold in lightly whipped cream, then add whisked egg whites and finally the gelatine. Pour mixture into souffle case and chill. Stand on large plate and decorate with chopped nuts, whipped cream, glacé cherries and angelica.

EVERYDAY THOUGHTS
for everyday living

"A kiss can be a comma, a question mark or an exclamation point. That's basic spelling that every woman ought to know."

Mistinguett

"We owe almost all our knowledge, not to those who have agreed, but to those who have differed."

C C Colton

"To know that we know what we know, and that we do not know what we do not know, that is true knowledge."

Henry David Thoreau

"As we acquire more knowledge, things do not become more comprehensible, but more mysterious."

Albert Schweitzer

Addresses • Addresses • Addresses • Addresses • Addresses • Addresses • Addresses

K

Name

✉

☎

Name

✉

☎

Name

✉

☎

Name

✉

☎

Name

✉

☎

Name

✉

☎

IN THE KITCHEN ~ INTERNATIONAL RECIPES

FROM HUNGARY

STUFFED MUSHROOMS WITH EGER SAUCE

Ingredients

Mushroom caps
1 tbsp lemon juice
goose liver paté (or similar)
beaten egg
breadcrumbs
$^1/_2$ tsp salt
deep fat or oil for frying

For the Eger (red wine) Sauce:

1 tbsp redcurrant jelly
$^1/_4$ pint lamb gravy or stock
$^1/_4$ pint red wine or port wine

Method

To make the sauce, heat all ingredients together until the jelly has melted. Boil mushroom caps in water with salt and lemon juice until just tender. Stuff with paté and sandwich 2 caps together. Coat with eggs then breadcrumbs, then deep fry for a few minutes until lightly browned. Drain and serve immediately with red wine sauce.

STUFFED PANCAKES HORTO BAGY STYLE

Ingredients

veal stew with paprika
pancakes
cream and sour cream to taste

Method

Prepare veal stew with paprika. Mince cooked meat and use to stuff pancakes. Pile into ovenproof dish and cover with sauce made from stew gravy, cream and sour cream. Serve hot.

HUNGARIAN APPLE PIE

Ingredients

1 lb cooking apples
4 oz butter
1-2 tbsp milk
6 oz plain flour
1 egg, separated
2 oz ground almonds
strawberry jam

Method

Stew apples in as little water as possible. Sieve flour, rub in butter and mix to a dough with egg yolk and milk. Leave in cool place for 30 mins. Line 7-inch sandwich tin with half the pastry and partly blind bake for 10 mins. Mix ground almonds with sugar. Spread pastry with jam and cover with half the almond mixture. Fold stiffly whisked egg white into apple and put in pie tin. Sprinkle rest of sugar and almond mixture on top and cover with remaining pastry. Brush with milk and sprinkle with sugar. Bake in a hot oven for 25-30 mins. Serve with cream.

EVERYDAY THOUGHTS
for everyday living

"The fruits of labour are the sweetest of all pleasures."

Luc de Vauvenargues

"Laughter has no foreign accent."

Paul Lowney

"The most wasted day is that in which we have not laughed."

Chamfort

"Learning is ever young, even in old age."

Aeschylus

"Learn as though you would never be able to master it; hold it as though you would be in fear of losing it."

Confucius

Addresses • Addresses • Addresses • Addresses • Addresses • Addresses • Addresses

L

Name

✉

☎

Name

✉

☎

Name

✉

☎

Name

✉

☎

Name

✉

☎

Name

✉

☎

IN THE KITCHEN ~ INTERNATIONAL RECIPES

FROM SCOTLAND

SCOTCH BROTH

Ingredients

- 1 lb boiling beef/neck of mutton
- 4 pints water
- 2 tbsp barley (pearl)
- 1 tsp salt
- 2 tbsp yellow split peas
- 2 tbsp dried green peas
- 2 carrots
- 2 leeks
- 3 tbsp swede, diced
- 1 onion
- ½ small cabbage
- 1 dsp finely chopped parsley

Method

Put the water, salt, peas, washed pearl barley and meat into a large saucepan. Slowly bring to the boil. Skim. Dice vegetables, shred the cabbage and add. Bring back to the boil and simmer for about 2 hours until the meat is cooked and the peas tender. Add parsley, salt and pepper.

EVERYDAY SCOTCH HAGGIS

Ingredients

- ½ lb ox liver
- 4 oz shredded suet
- 1 onion
- 4 oz oatmeal, pinhead
- 2 pinches black pepper
- 1 teacup water
- ¾ dsp salt

Method

In a small saucepan put liver, onion and water. Boil for 15 minutes. Toast the oatmeal for a few minutes in the oven until it is light brown. Mince the liver and onion. Mix everything together with the liquid and seasoning. Serve with swedes and mashed potatoes.

PETTICOAT TAILS

Ingredients

- 12 oz margarine/butter
- 18 oz plain flour
- 9 oz icing sugar
- 1 tbsp castor sugar

Method

Cream the butter and sift in the icing sugar. Beat the flour in with the icing sugar, adding sufficient water to make a firm dough. Roll the dough out thinly into a large square. Cut it into 2-inch triangles. Place the triangles on a greased baking sheet and bake at 325°F (or equivalent temperature) for 30 minutes. Remove from oven and dust with castor sugar while they are still hot. Leave the triangles on the tray to cool.

EVERYDAY THOUGHTS
for everyday living

"We make a living by what we get, but we make a life by what we give."

Norman MacEwan

"It is not the years in your life but the life in your years that counts!"

Adlai Stevenson

"The love we give away is the only love we keep."

Elbert Hubbard

"Treasure the love you receive above all. It will survive long after your gold and good health have vanished."

Og Mandino

"Who, being loved, is poor?"

Oscar Wilde

Addresses • Addresses • Addresses • Addresses • Addresses • Addresses • Addresses • Addresses

L

Name

✉

☎

Name

✉

☎

Name

✉

☎

Name

✉

☎

Name

✉

☎

Name

✉

☎

FRIENDS & FOOD PREFERENCES

Little can be so disheartening to the cook to learn that a meal that has been hours in the preparation is poison to one of the guests - maybe he or she is a vegetarian, allergic to eggs, detests olives . . . ! Avoid uncomfortable situations by keeping a record of your friends' most important food preferences.

Friend ....
Allergies/ ....
Dislikes ....

Friend ....
Allergies/ ....
Dislikes ....

Friend ....
Allergies/ ....
Dislikes ....

Friend ....
Allergies/ ....
Dislikes ....

Friend ....
Allergies/ ....
Dislikes ....

Friend ....
Allergies/ ....
Dislikes ....

Friend ....
Allergies/ ....
Dislikes ....

Friend ....
Allergies/ ....
Dislikes ....

Friend ....
Allergies/ ....
Dislikes ....

Friend ....
Allergies/ ....
Dislikes ....

Friend ....
Allergies/ ....
Dislikes ....

Friend ....
Allergies/ ....
Dislikes ....

Notes ....

....

....

EVERYDAY THOUGHTS

for everyday living

"Marriage is an empty box.
It remains empty unless you put
in more than you take out."

Author Unidentified

"Married couples who love each
other tell each other a thousand
things without talking."

Chinese Proverb

"Often the difference between a
successful marriage and a mediocre
one consists of leaving about three
or four things a day unsaid."

Harlan Miller

"Marriage is three parts love and
seven parts forgiveness of sins."

Langdon Mitchell

"There is no more lovely, friendly
and charming relationship,
communion or company than
a good marriage."

Martin Luther

Addresses • Addresses • Addresses • Addresses • Addresses • Addresses • Addresses

M

Name

Name

Name

Name

Name

Name

DINNER PARTY RECORDS

Date/Occasion

Guests

Menu

Notes

Date/Occasion

Guests

Menu

Notes

EVERYDAY THOUGHTS
for everyday living

"Memory is the treasury and guardian of all things."

Cicero

"God gave us memories that we might have roses in December."

James M Barrie

"The greatest mistake you can make in life is to be continually fearing you will make one."

Elbert Hubbard

"He who makes no mistakes never makes anything."

English Proverb

"The shortest mistakes are always the best."

J B Molière

Addresses • Addresses • Addresses • Addresses • Addresses • Addresses • Addresses

M

Name

✉

☎

Name

✉

☎

Name

✉

☎

Name

✉

☎

Name

✉

☎

Name

✉

☎

DINNER PARTY RECORDS

Date/Occasion ....

Guests

....
....
....
....
....
....
....

Menu

....
....
....
....
....
....
....

Notes ....

....
....

Date/Occasion ....

Guests

....
....
....
....
....
....
....

Menu

....
....
....
....
....
....
....

Notes ....

....
....

EVERYDAY THOUGHTS
for everyday living

"What's in a name?
That which we call a rose,
By any other name would
smell as sweet."

Shakespeare: Romeo & Juliet

"A nation reveals itself not only by the men it produces but also by the men it honours, the men it remembers."

John F Kennedy

"Those things are better which are perfected by nature than those which are finished by art."

Cicero

"God made the beauties of nature like a child playing in the sand."

Ascribed to Apollonius of Tyana

"Better is a neighbour that is near than a brother far off."

Proverbs 27:10

Addresses • Addresses • Addresses • Addresses • Addresses • Addresses • Addresses

N

Name

Name

Name

Name

Name

Name

DINNER PARTY RECORDS

Date/Occasion ....

Guests

....
....
....
....
....
....
....

Menu

....
....
....
....
....
....
....

Notes ....

....

....

Date/Occasion ....

Guests

....
....
....
....
....
....
....

Menu

....
....
....
....
....
....
....

Notes ....

....

....

EVERYDAY THOUGHTS
for everyday living

"When your neighbour's house is afire,
your own property is at stake."

Horace

"Night is the mother of counsels."

George Herbert

"The day is done, and the darkness
Falls from the wings of Night,
As a feather is wafted downward
From an eagle in his flight."

Longfellow

"Be noble! and the nobleness that lies
In other men, sleeping, but never dead,
Will rise in majesty to meet thine own."

James Russell Lowell

"How sad would be November if we
had no knowledge of the spring!"

Edwin Way Teale

Addresses • Addresses • Addresses • Addresses • Addresses • Addresses • Addresses • Addresses

N

Name

✉

☎

Name

✉

☎

Name

✉

☎

Name

✉

☎

Name

✉

☎

Name

✉

☎

Animal Hair

Use sellotape to remove animal hair from clothes, furniture etc. Simply wrap the sellotape around your fingers (sticky side outward) and rub over the hairs.

Ants

You can discourage ants in the house by sprinkling bicarbonate of soda or powdered borax of cloves on shelves and in drawers.

Ash

Do not empty these into a wastepaper basket as they can easily start a fire. A large tin is much more suitable. To prevent cigarette ends from burning in an ashtray and to reduce the smell of stale tobacco, coat the bottom of the ashtray with baking powder.

Baking Tins

To discourage a new baking tin from rusting, rub it inside and out with lard and place it in an oven at moderate heat for forty-five minutes. When cool wipe thoroughly with a paper towel. To remove rust from tinware rub with half a raw potato that has been dipped in scouring powder. Rinse and then dry - ideally in an oven.

Ball Point Pens

If a ballpoint pen doesn't work try warming the point gently with a match or by pouring boiling water over it.

Barbecue

To maximise the heat line your barbecue with tin-foil, shiny side up. Use left over brewed coffee to clean the barbecue set.

Baths

If you have unsightly stains on your bath or wash basin due to a dripping tap, try rubbing with a paste made of lemon juice and salt and rinsing well. Failing this, try rubbing them with a toothbrush using a paste of cream of tartar and peroxide and then rinsing.

Books

To keep your books in good condition do not place them tight against a wall, but leave a couple of centimetres gap to enable the air to circulate around them. Also, make sure they are kept upright and not leaning at an angle as this would be bad for their bindings.

If the pages of a book are torn slightly, place them in position and smear lightly with the white of an egg, leaving the book open to dry.

Carpet tape is useful when trying to repair the spine of a book.

Bottles

Stick an adhesive plaster over the cork of the bottle containing liquid when packing to help prevent accidents. It is also advisable to pack bottles between soft items.

Bottles are best emptied by shaking them in a circular motion.

EVERYDAY THOUGHTS
for everyday living

"The woman who obeys her
husband rules him."

Spanish Proverb

"An old man loved is winter
with flowers."

German Proverb

"Our opinions are less important than the spirit and temper with which they possess us, and even good opinions are worth very little unless we hold them in a broad, intelligent, and spacious way."

John Morley

"Every man values himself more than all the rest of men, but he always values others' opinions of himself more than his own."

Marcus Aurelius

Addresses • Addresses • Addresses • Addresses • Addresses • Addresses • Addresses

O

Name

Name

Name

Name

Name

Name

If you find difficulty unscrewing a bottle or container give a firm tap to the bottom of the container.

Remove strong odours from bottles by filling them with a mixture of cold water and four teaspoons of dry mustard and leaving them to stand for a least half a day before rinsing well.

Bread Boards

If your wooden bread board is warped, place it on a flat surface and cover it with a wet cloth, leaving it for at least 24 hours.

Brooms

When a broom handle does not fit anymore then wrap with adhesive tape and screw the handle back into the socket. This should help keep it in place.

Candles

To increase the life span of candles keep them in the freezer for a few hours before use.

To make candles fit into candle sticks dip the end in hot water until it is soft enough to fit into the required size.

Wash the candle stick holder in soapy water with a few drops of ammonia to remove the wax.

Car

To prevent bumping your car in a tight garage attach an old tyre to the wall.

To clean a very dirty car use a mixture of methylated spirit and water (1 unit of methylated spirit to 8 units of water). Do not rinse. This should leave your car shining.

Carpets

When choosing a carpet ask to see it flat on the floor. The colour might look quite different when the carpet is displayed rolled vertically.

To restore the life to carpet pile which has been flattened by furniture legs, place several layers of wet cloth onto the area. Then hold a hot iron lightly on top of the cloth. The steam should bring back the bounce to the carpet which can then be fluffed up using a nail brush.

China

Protect your best china plates from chips and cracks by alternating them with paper plates or corrugated paper when storing them or when packing them.

Cooking Smells

Get rid of unwanted cooking smells by boiling one teaspoon of ground cinnamon or ground cloves in a ¼ litre of water for fifteen minutes.

Cork

Cork expands. If it does not fit back into the bottle then place it in boiling water for a few minutes until it becomes soft. It will then fit easily back into the bottle.

Crystal

To give a real sparkle to your crystal add a few drops of ammonia to the washing water and vinegar to the rinsing water.

EVERYDAY THOUGHTS
for everyday living

"One often contradicts an opinion when it is really only the tone in which it has been presented that is unsympathetic."

Nietzsche

"When we stop to think, we often miss our opportunity."

Publilius Syrus

"A wise man will make more opportunities than he finds."

Francis Bacon

"An optimist sees an opportunity in every calamity: a pessimist sees a calamity in every opportunity."

Author Unidentified

"Originality does not consist in saying what no one has ever said before, but in saying exactly what you think yourself."

James Fitz-James Stephen

Addresses • Addresses • Addresses • Addresses • Addresses • Addresses • Addresses

O

Name

Name

Name

Name

Name

Name

HANDY HINTS

Dampness
To determine whether dampness is caused by condensation or is coming from outside, attach a piece of silver foil to the affected area. If moisture appears on the front surface then this is caused by condensation in the room and you should look for better ways of ventilating the room. If, however, the foil is wet on the side of the wall, the damp comes from the outside and you should seek professional help.

Decorating
When you have decorated a room, make sure you keep a note of the number of rolls of wallpaper or tins of paint that you used, so that when you come to redecorating, you will know exactly what you need.

Dishwashers
Pour 4 heaped tablespoons of bicarbonate of soda through the bottom rack of your dishwasher and put it on the rinse cycle to refresh the smell.

Doors
Silence a creaky door by rubbing soap along the hinges.

Drawers
If you have trouble opening tight fitting drawers, rub soap or candle wax along the upper edges to lubricate them.

Drilling
To stop the drill from slipping when drilling a hole into metal or ceramic tiles, cover the mark with adhesive tape, drill through it and then remove the tape.

When drilling into the ceiling, drill through the base of an old squash bottle or transparent plastic container and this will catch the chips and stop them from going into your eyes.

Easter Eggs
Use natural products to dye Easter eggs: beetroot juice will make a red dye, saffron will give you yellow, and spinach juice will produce a green colour.

Egg Boxes
Cardboard or fibre egg boxes are ideal for growing seeds. When the shoots are ready for planting, just bury the entire tray. The roots will not be disturbed and the tray will disintegrate after a while.

Electric-Wire
When fitting a plug it is often difficult to cut the rubber which encompasses the wire without cutting the copper thread. If you warm the rubber with a match you will be able to strip it very easily with your fingers.

Enamel
If your enamel is cracked and the cracks become dirty, make a thick paste of French chalk and water and coat the enamel with it. Leave it until the paste dries out and begins to crack and then brush off. Repeat until the cracks come clean.

Erasers
Washing-up liquid effectively cleans dirty erasers.

Felt-Tipped Pens
If your felt-tip pen seems to have run out, try

EVERYDAY THOUGHTS
for everyday living

"If we live in peace ourselves,
we in turn may bring peace to others.
A peaceable man does more good
than a learned one."

Thomas À Kempis

"Perfection is attained by slow degrees;
it requires the hand of time."

Voltaire

"By perseverance the snail
reached the Ark."

C H Spurgeon

"Philosophy triumphs easily over past,
and over future evils, but present evils
triumph over philosophy."

François de la Rochefoucauld

"The entire world would perish,
if pity were not to limit anger."

Seneca the Elder

Addresses • Addresses • Addresses • Addresses • Addresses • Addresses • Addresses

P

Name

☎

Name

☎

Name

☎

Name

☎

Name

☎

Name

☎

dipping the tip in a little vinegar - this should give it a new lease of life. Store felt-tip pens tip downwards with the cap on so that they are always ready to use.

Finger Nails
If you want to take care of your nails, never cut them with scissors as this can cause them to split. File them with an emery board - from the sides up to the tip (and never in a see-saw movement) - as this is softer than a metal file.

Fireplaces
If you are lighting a fire in a chimney which has not been used for some time and which may be damp, first burn a creased sheet of newspaper in the grate. This should remove the moisture from the chimney and help you get the best out of the fireplace.

When burning a fire, do not burn coloured magazines or newspaper as the coloured ink will give off some lead vapour when burning.

Flies
A pleasant way of discouraging flies is by placing cotton wool balls sprinkled with a few drops of lavender oil on saucers around the room. Basil or mint grown in pots on the windowsill or in a window box is also a sweet smelling way of deterring flies.

Floors
Talcum powder sprinkled between floorboards will help to stop them from squeaking.

Flowers
If you are picking flowers from the garden, do not do it during the warmest part of the day as the flowers will not last long. Pick them in the early morning or early evening if you want them to last longer.

Foil
Wrap food tightly in kitchen foil for storing but loosely for cooking.

Framing
Insert kitchen foil behind the picture when framing to prevent damage from damp.

Freezer
When you have defrosted your freezer rub the inside with glycerine. Next time you come to defrost it you should find that the ice will come away easily.

To stop packages from sticking to the freezer walls or bottom, do not put them straight back into the freezer after defrosting but leave the freezer empty for half an hour first.

Furniture
When it is exposed to direct sunlight, polished furniture will permanently lose its veneer. To

EVERYDAY THOUGHTS
for everyday living

"Poetry is the opening and closing of a door, leaving those who look through to guess about what is seen during a moment."

Carl Sandburg

"It is not the man who has little, but he who desires more, that is poor."

Seneca

"The sole advantage of power is that you can do more good."

Baltasar Gracián

"Prejudice is the child of ignorance."

William Hazlitt

"Problems are opportunities in work clothes."

Henry Kaiser

"To the pure all things are pure."

Titus 1:15

Addresses • Addresses • Addresses • Addresses • Addresses • Addresses • Addresses

P

Name

✉

☎

Name

✉

☎

Name

✉

☎

Name

✉

☎

Name

✉

☎

Name

✉

☎

avoid lasting damage, either position the piece of furniture elsewhere, or keep it covered with a cloth.

Fuses

Keep a torch and a card of fuse wire beside the fuse box in case of an emergency.

Garden Tools

To remove rust from your garden tools use wire wool dipped in turpentine.

Garlic

To remove the smell of garlic from your breath try chewing some fresh mint, a coffee bean, a stalk of parsley or celery or some cardamom seeds!

Gift Wrap

When you are wrapping large numbers of presents, at Christmas for example or at a children's party, try using attractive leftover wallpaper which makes a far cheaper alternative to gift wrap.

Glasses

If two glasses have stuck together and you are finding it difficult to separate them, stand the bottom glass in hot (not boiling) water and fill the top one with cold water. This should cause them to separate without damaging them.

To get rid of small chips around the rim of a glass, rub them with fine sandpaper until smooth.

Stand a silver spoon in a glass or jar to prevent it from cracking when boiling water is poured into it.

Glue

Fit a piece of candle on the top of a glue bottle and use it as a stopper to close the bottle. As glue does not stick to candle wax you should no longer have any problems when you come to open it.

Grass

To prevent grass from growing between the cracks in your paving stones or path, sprinkle salt in them, or pour on very salted boiling water.

Greenfly

You can help to discourage greenfly by planting garlic around the plants that attract the greenfly. When the garlic starts sprouting, keep the shoots cut back.

Gutters

A piece of chicken wire placed over the top of your gutter will effectively prevent falling leaves from blocking it.

Hangers

If you have a skirt without any loops and are short of special hangers, wind a rubber band around each end of an ordinary hanger to prevent the skirt from falling off, or put two clothes pegs on an ordinary wire hanger.

EVERYDAY THOUGHTS
for everyday living

"Quarrels would not last long if the fault was only on one side."

François de la Rochefoucauld

"The second word makes the quarrel."

Japanese Proverb

"Most quarrels amplify a misunderstanding."

André Gide

"You can make up a quarrel but it will always show where it was patched."

Edgar Watson Howe

"Better is a handful with quietness, than both the hands full with travails and vexation of spirit."

Ecclesiastes 4:6

"No wealth is like the quiet mind."

Author Unidentified

Addresses • Addresses • Addresses • Addresses • Addresses • Addresses • Addresses

Q

Name

✉

☎

Name

✉

☎

Name

✉

☎

Name

✉

☎

Name

✉

☎

Name

✉

☎

Hard Water Deposits

If you find hard water deposits in jugs, bottles, vases or glasses etc., fill the object with malt vinegar and leave it for a few hours or as long as necessary. Then rub off with a fine wire scouring pad and rinse thoroughly. The vinegar can be reused.

Hose

To make the hose fit easily onto the tap rub the inside of the hose with some soap. The soap will quickly dry when the hose is fitted.

Hot-Water bottles

When filling a hot-water bottle lie it flat on its back holding the neck upright. This will prevent the water splashing due to air-bubbles in the bottle. Add a little salt to the water to keep it warm longer.

Insects

By hanging a fresh bunch of stinging nettles in front of any open windows or doors, you can discourage flies and wasps from invading your house.

Ironing

Starch can be removed from the bottom of your iron by sprinkling a piece of paper with some fine kitchen salt and rubbing the iron over it until the base becomes smooth again, or by rubbing the base with half a lemon dipped in fine kitchen salt.

A few drops of your favourite toilet water mixed with the water in the iron or sprinkled first on the ironing board will perfume your linen lightly.

Ivory

Very dirty ivory can be cleaned by leaving the item to soak for a few hours in milk and then washing it with warm soapy water.

To keep small pieces of ivory white, place them in the direct sunlight. Alternatively, to colour a piece of ivory which looks too new, dip it in strong tea or coffee. Do not leave it to soak but keep dipping it in and out until the desired effect is reached. Dry and polish.

Jars

Leave a few drops of bleach in a glass jar to remove strong fish or pickle smells. You will have to leave the bleach in for at least twelve hours.

If you make some small holes in the lid of a jam jar or other glass screw-topped jar with a nail or skewer, you can use it as a cheap flour dredger or as a water sprinkler when ironing.

EVERYDAY THOUGHTS
for everyday living

"It is reason that produces everything: virtue, genius, wit, talent, and taste. What is virtue? Reason in practise. Talent? Reason enveloped in glory. Wit? Reason which is chastely expressed. Taste is nothing else than reason delicately put in force, and genius is reason in its most sublime form."

M J de Chenier

"Opportunities flit by while we sit regretting the chances we have lost, and the happiness that comes to us we heed not, because of the happiness that is gone."

Jerome K Jerome

"To regret deeply is to live afresh."

Thoreau

"Work is the price which is paid for reputation."

Baltasar Gracian

Addresses • Addresses • Addresses • Addresses • Addresses • Addresses • Addresses

R

Name

Name

Name

Name

Name

Name

Jar Labels
Do not label your jars until the contents have cooled, otherwise the labels will come unstuck.

Jewellery
If you want to give a quick shine to gold jewellery, rub the item with a ball of soft bread. Likewise if you want an item of silver jewellery to shine, rub it with half a lemon and then rinse before drying.

To loosen or remove a ring which is stuck on your finger, wash your hands with soap and water and try to take the ring off while the soap is still on your hands.

Kettles
Place a marble in your kettle to prevent it from furring. To defur a kettle fill it with water and put the kettle in your freezer. When it defrosts the ice will pull the fur of the sides. Alternatively, pour in a small quantity of vinegar (enough to cover the element where applicable), bring it to the boil then agitate it. Leave it to cool and then rinse thoroughly. It may be necessary to repeat these processes several times.

Keys
Covering a rusty key with turpentine and leaving it to soak for a couple of hours before rubbing and drying it should bring its shine back.

Knitwear
To prevent your knitwear from stretching when you are washing it in the washing machine, place it first inside a pillowcase.

Leather Shoes
When drying leather shoes or boots, never be tempted to do so quickly in front of the fire as the leather will harden and will be more likely to crack.

Lids
If you cannot unscrew a lid, place the jar in boiling water for a few minutes. It should then become loose and easy to unscrew.

Light Bulbs
You can delicately scent your room by rubbing just a few drops of your favourite perfume onto a light bulb. A pleasant smell will be emitted when the light bulb is on.

Linen
To prevent fine linen which is not in constant use from becoming discoloured and yellow, wrap it in blue tissue paper.

Linoleum
Unsightly black marks on linoleum floors can be removed quite simply by using a pencil-eraser. A few drops of paraffin in the water when washing will help make linoleum shine.

Lipstick
When you are testing a lipstick for colour, the best place to try it is on the cushion of your finger, where the skin is pinkish, like the lips.

Locks
When you cannot get your key to turn in a lock and it seems to be jammed, rub the key with vaseline, or, failing that, butter or margarine. This should help to ease the lock.

EVERYDAY THOUGHTS
for everyday living

"Respect a man, he will do the more."

James Howell

"If you have some respect for people as they are, you can be more effective in helping them to become better than they are."

John W Gardner

"He that can take rest is greater than he that can take cities."

Benjamin Franklin

"It is better to be miserable and rich than it is to be miserable and poor."

Author Unidentified

"The rich man is not one who is in possession of much, but one who gives much."

St. John Chrysostom

Addresses • Addresses • Addresses • Addresses • Addresses • Addresses • Addresses

R

Name

Name

Name

Name

Name

Name

A lubricating effect can also be achieved by rubbing a key all over with pencil lead and working it in the lock several times. This will help to keep the lock in good working order.

MATS
You can help to prevent the edges of a mat from curling up by pasting some very thick starch along the edge and then ironing over some brown paper with a fairly hot iron.

MATCHES
A damp match can be made to light by coating the tip in nail varnish. You do not even have to wait for the nail varnish to dry before striking it. An alternative is to rub it against the bristles of a brush.

MICROWAVE OVENS
You can help to remove stubborn and unpleasant cooking smells from inside a microwave oven by placing a teacup containing 3 parts water to 1 part lemon juice or vinegar inside it and cooking for eight to ten minutes on the lowest setting. Wipe the oven dry afterwards.

MIRRORS
If, before you run your bath, you rub the bathroom mirror with a few drops of shampoo, this will help prevent it from steaming up.

MOTHS
Small muslin bags filled with aromatic plants placed in your wardrobe and drawers will deter moths and will make your clothes smell nice at the same time.

NAILS
When hammering small nails use a hairslide as a holder or stick plasticine over the area you wish to hammer the nail into. This will hold the nail in position and will protect your fingers.

To prevent cracking the plaster when hammering in nails, first stick a piece of sellotape or masking tape to the wall, then hammer the nail in through the tape.

When trying to remove a nail which has been painted over, first soften the paint by holding a lighted match just below it, being careful not to burn the wall.

NAIL VARNISH
You can keep the top of a bottle of nail varnish from sticking and becoming difficult to open by spreading a little vaseline on the grooves.

Storing the bottle in the fridge will prevent the nail varnish from getting a sticky consistency and it will also help the varnish to last longer.

If the varnish thickens, it can be brought back to a better consistency by adding just a few drops of nail varnish remover.

NEWSPAPER
Roll a newspaper into a long thin tube, knotted in the middle, when you are lighting a fire.

OVENS
Next time you clean your oven, after cleaning and drying it rub it all over with a paste made of bicarbonate of soda and water. This should make it easier to wipe clean next time around.

EVERYDAY THOUGHTS
for everyday living

"Silence is as full of potential wisdom and wit as the unhewn marble of great sculpture."

Aldous Huxley

"The art of art, the glory of expression and the sunshine of the light of letters, is simplicity."

Walt Whitman

"Sincerity is the highest compliment you can pay."

Ralph Waldo Emerson

"Sorrow is better than fear . . . Fear is a journey, a terrible journey, but sorrow is at least an arriving."

Alan Paton: Cry the Beloved Country

"Our joys as winged dreams do fly, Why then should sorrow last?"

Thomas Percy

S

Name

✉

☎

Name

✉

☎

Name

✉

☎

Name

✉

☎

Name

✉

☎

Name

✉

☎

PAINT
When selecting a single colour for the walls of a room, always choose one a shade lighter than you want, as paint tends to look darker once it is on the wall.

To keep the top of a paint tin clean, when painting place a paper plate over the top of the tin with the middle cut out. This way all the drops will land on the plate and not on the tin, and the plate can simply be discarded after you have finished painting.

The strong smell left in your house after you have been painting can be avoided by using a mixture of one tablespoon of vanilla essence to two pints paint when you are painting. Or while painting, try adding a couple of tablespoons of ammonia to one or two shallow containers of water placed in the room you are working on - this should stop the smell from spreading around the house.

PAINTBRUSHES
Dried out brushes can be restored to life by immersing them in hot vinegar, while errant bristles can be encouraged to return to their proper place by spraying the brush head with hairspray, smoothing and leaving to dry.

PAINT TUBES
To get a stubborn cap off a small tube of artist's paint, try holding a lighted match under the cap for just a few seconds.

PAN
Before using a new pan, boil some vinegar in it for a few minutes to prevent food from sticking.

PARCELS
When you are wrapping a parcel using string, first dip the string in warm water and then tie the knot. When the string dries it will shrink, leaving you with a tight knot.

PIANOS
Do not place a lot of books or ornaments on the top of a piano as it will deaden the tone. If a piano key stays down when it is struck then it is a sign of dampness.

Ivory keys will become yellowed more quickly if the lid of the piano is kept down, as ivory yellows more in the dark.

PINS
If you keep a small magnet in your pin box, then if you drop it the keys will be more likely to cluster around the magnet, making it easier to collect them.

PLASTIC BOTTLES
For easier and more compact disposal of your

EVERYDAY THOUGHTS
for everyday living

"It is excellent
To have a giant's strength,
but it is tyrannous
To use it like a giant."

Shakespeare: Measure for Measure

"The true measure of success is
not what you have, but what
you can do without."

Author Unidentified

"He has achieved success who
has lived well, laughed often
and loved much."

Bessie Anderson Stanley

"Know how sublime a thing it is
to suffer and be strong."

Longfellow

"Pity may represent little more than the
impersonal concern which prompts the
mailing of a cheque, but true sympathy
is the personal concern which
demands the giving of one's soul."

Martin Luther King

Addresses • Addresses • Addresses • Addresses • Addresses • Addresses • Addresses

S

Name

✉

☎

Name

✉

☎

Name

✉

☎

Name

✉

☎

Name

✉

☎

Name

✉

☎

plastic bottles, pour a small quantity of boiling water into the bottle. This will cause it to become soft and to collapse, making it easier to crush the bottle in your hands.

Plasticine
A quick substitute for plasticine for children to play with can be made by making a dough with flour, water and salt. This can be coloured with a little paprika or mustard powder to make it more attractive, and it will stay soft if stored in a sealed plastic bag.

If you do not want to use a trellis and yet still wish your ivy to grow up the wall, encourage it by sticking it to the wall from time to time with plasticine.

Plasters
If you find removing sticking plaster from your skin painful, first rub baby oil over the plaster. You should find it easier to remove.

Refrigerators
A piece of charcoal placed inside your fridge will absorb the smells of strong food such as fish and cheese and will only need to be replaced every five-to-six months.

If your fridge is noisy it could simply be that it is not standing on a level surface.

Rubber Gloves
As hands sweat a lot in rubber gloves, they may become damp and smell unpleasant. Avoid this by dusting the inside of the gloves with talc when you use them and by washing the insides from time to time. It will also help if you dry the gloves inside out after you have used them.

Rubbish
To keep dogs and cats away from your rubbish sprinkle pure ammonia over the bags.

Rugs
To keep a rug from slipping or wrinkling on a carpet or shiny floor, stick some plastic stick-ons, commonly used for the bath, on the underside of the rug. Alternatively, you could sew or glue pieces of carpet, pile downwards, under the corners of the rug.

Rust
Rust on utensils can be removed by rubbing the stains with a cork dipped in olive oil. Rust stains on metal will sometimes disappear when rubbed with half a raw onion.

Scissors
To sharpen your scissors cut a sheet of emery paper into small pieces.

Shine
Black or dark coloured clothes often become shiny with wear. This can be alleviated by brushing the shiny part with black coffee - half a teacup of strong black coffee to half a teacup of water. Then press with a cloth. Alternatively, you could rub the article with a piece of clean cloth dampened with turpentine or white spirit. The smell will soon disappear.

Shoes
When buying shoes, wait until the afternoon. Your feet tend to be relaxed first thing in the

EVERYDAY THOUGHTS
for everyday living

"Waste not fresh tears over old griefs."

Euripides

"There's no seeing one's way through tears."

English Proverb

"Why comes temptation
but for man to meet
And master and make crouch
beneath his foot,
And so be pedestalled in
triumph?"

Robert Browning

"I can resist everything except temptation."

Oscar Wilde: Lady Windermere's Fan

"Our life is what our thoughts make it."

Marcus Aurelius

Addresses • Addresses • Addresses • Addresses • Addresses • Addresses • Addresses

T

Name

✉

☎

Name

✉

☎

Name

✉

☎

Name

✉

☎

Name

✉

☎

Name

✉

☎

morning after a night's sleep but may swell slightly during the day, so if you buy your shoes early in the morning you may find that they pinch you in the evening.

Remove the odour from smelly shoes by sprinkling a tablespoon of bicarbonate of soda inside each shoe and leaving it overnight.

When drying wet shoes, stuff them with newspaper to help them keep their shape.

Shower Curtains

To prevent mildew on your cloth shower curtains, soak them for half an hour in a strong solution of salted water, then hang them up to dry. Rubbing the curtains with bicarbonate of soda will also help remove mildew.

Slugs

One of the less offensive ways of killing slugs is by distributing bran around the garden, which they are attracted to but which kills them. (The bran will also attract snails, who will assemble around it making it easy to collect them).

Alternatively, you can entice the slugs with a glass of beer left in the garden overnight.

Smoke

To prevent a room from becoming smoky when people are smoking in it, try lighting a few candles, or strategically arrange a few small containers filled with vinegar. This should help to eliminate the smoke from the room.

Stains

When removing a stain, work from the edge of the stain inwards. This will help prevent the stain from spreading.

Stamps

When you wish to remove an unused stamp from an envelope without damaging it, submerge the corner of the envelope with the stamp on it in boiling water for a few minutes. The stamp should then come off easily and can be left to dry.

Another method is to wet the back of the stamp inside the envelope with lighter fluid.

Sticky Labels

Stubborn sticky labels on glass or china can be removed with nail-varnish remover, cooking oil, turpentine or white spirit.

Thermos Flasks

To clean a stained thermos flask put three tablespoons of bicarbonate of soda into it and fill up with warm water. Agitate it and leave to stand for quarter of an hour. Then rinse and leave to dry.

Stubborn coffee smells and stains can be eliminated by pouring in a cup of boiling water and one tablespoon of raw rice. Shake the flask for a few minutes and then rinse.

If you will not be using your flask for a while,

EVERYDAY THOUGHTS
for everyday living

"Human thought, like God, makes the world in its own image."

Adam Clayton Powell

"Nimble thought can jump both sea and land."

Shakespeare: Sonnets

"Tolerance implies no lack of commitment to one's own beliefs. Rather it condemns the oppression of persecution of others."

John F Kennedy

"The heaviest baggage for a traveller is an empty purse."

English Proverb

"In travelling: a man must carry knowledge with him, if he would bring home knowledge."

Samuel Johnson

Name

✉

☎

Name

✉

☎

Name

✉

☎

Name

✉

☎

Name

✉

☎

Name

✉

☎

pop a couple of lumps of sugar into it to prevent mouldy smells developing.

Thread
To prevent your double thread tangling when sewing, knot the ends separately instead of together.

Toilet Bowls
You can easily remove hard water marks inside the toilet bowl by pouring three teacups of vinegar into the bowl and allowing it to soak for a few hours before brushing and flushing.

Vacuum Flask
When storing a vacuum flask empty, leave the top off to avoid getting a musty smell.

If the flask does smell musty, fill it with a mixture of warm water and two tablespoons of white vinegar, leaving it to stand for several minutes before shaking and rinsing well. If this fails to eliminate the smell, try a mixture of hot water and one and a half tablespoons of bicarbonate of soda. Leave it for at least four hours and rinse well.

Wallpaper
When storing your rolls of wallpaper, keep them horizontal, not upright as the ends are more likely to get damaged if they are left standing up.

Washing
To prevent dark clothes from picking up fluff when washed with other items, turn inside out before placing them in the washing machine.

Washing-up Liquid Bottle
A clean washing-up liquid bottle filled with water is an ideal watering can for your house plants, enabling you to control the water and to avoid spillages.

Waste-Disposal Unit
To clean your waste disposal unit, sprinkle a dozen or so ice cubes with scouring powder and pass them through it, finishing with a few orange or lemon peels.

Watches
If the glass of your watch gets misted up, turn it over and wear the glass next to your skin for a little while. The warmth from your skin will help to clear the mist.

Watering Plants
If you are going away on holiday and can find no one to water your plants, keep them moist by soaking the soil thoroughly and then placing the plant and pot, still dripping, in a polythene bag. Close the bag tightly and place in a position where the plant will receive indirect sunlight.

Weight
When you are keeping an eye on your weight, weigh yourself at the same time of the day once a week. This will give you a truer idea of any weight loss or gain by counteracting any daily fluctuations.

Windows
When painting window frames, protect the glass from paint by laying strips of dampened newspaper along the edges and in the corners. These will be easy to remove afterwards.

EVERYDAY THOUGHTS
for everyday living

"Uncertainty is the worst of all evils until the moment when reality makes us regret uncertainty."

Alphonse Karr

"All uncertainty is fruitful . . . so long as it is accompanied by the wish to understand."

Antonio Machado

"Understanding is the beginning of approving."

André Gide

"In what we really understand we reason but little."

William Hazlitt

"Between our birth and death we may touch understanding as a moth brushes a window with its wing."

Christopher Fry

Addresses • Addresses • Addresses • Addresses • Addresses • Addresses • Addresses

U

Name

Name

Name

Name

Name

Name

HANDY HINTS

Wool

Thick wool can be difficult to thread - if you damp it with saliva it tends to just bounce back. Instead, try rolling the tip on a wet piece of soap and then rub it between your fingers. The ply should then stick together.

Wrinkles in Clothes

If you do not have access to an iron, for example if you are travelling, hang the clothes in the bathroom and fill the bath with hot water. If you close the door and leave for a while, the steam should help remove the creases from your garments.

Zips

A zip can be helped to run smoothly by rubbing it with a little soft soap, some candle wax or a pencil lead.

My Own Notes

EVERYDAY THOUGHTS
for everyday living

"To understand all is to pardon all."
[Tout comprendre rend très indulgent.]

Anna Louise de Stael

"A man should always consider how much he has more than he wants, and how much more unhappy he might be than he really is."

Joseph Addison

"When spiders' webs unite, they can tie up a lion."

Ethiopian Proverb

"Not vain the weakest, if their force unite."

Homer

"Once men are caught up in an event they cease to be afraid. Only the unknown frightens men."

Saint-Exupéry

Addresses • Addresses • Addresses • Addresses • Addresses • Addresses • Addresses

U

Name

✉

☎

Name

✉

☎

Name

✉

☎

Name

✉

☎

Name

✉

☎

Name

✉

☎

USEFUL INFORMATION

TEMPERATURE

F'heit	22°F	32°F	41°F	59°F	68°F	86°F
Celsius	-5°C	0°C	5°C	15°C	20°C	30°C

Conversion Formulae

$C = \frac{5}{9}(F - 32)$

$F = \frac{9}{5}(C + 32)$

ROMAN NUMERALS

I	= 1		XVI	=	16
II	=	2	XVII	=	17
III	=	3	XVIII	=	18
IV	=	4	XIX	=	19
V	=	5	XX	=	20
VI	=	6	XXX	=	30
VII	=	7	XL	=	40
VIII	=	8	L	=	50
IX	=	9	LX	=	60
X	=	10	LXX	=	70
XI	=	11	LXXX	=	80
XII	=	12	XC	=	90
XIII	=	13	C	=	100
XIV	=	14	D	=	500
XV	=	15	M	=	1000

WIND SPEEDS

1	7 mph light wind
2	11 mph light breeze
3	16 mph gentle breeze
4	20 mph moderate breeze
5	25 mph fresh breeze
6	30 mph strong breeze
7	35 mph moderate gale
8	45 mph fresh gale
9	50 mph strong gale
10	60 mph whole gale
11	70 mph storm
12	80 mph hurricane

~ INTERNATIONAL PAPER SIZES (A SERIES) ~

SIZE	MILIMETRES	INCHES
A0	841 x 1189	33.1 x 46.8
A1	594 x 841	23.4 x 33.1
A2	420 x 594	16.5 x 23.4
A3	297 x 420	11.7 x 16.5
A4	210 x 297	8.3 x 11.7
A5	148 x 210	5.8 x 8.3
A6	105 x 148	4.1 x 5.8
A7	74 x 105	2.9 x 4.1

EVERYDAY THOUGHTS
for everyday living

"It's not hard to make decisions when you know what your values are."

Roy Disney

"There are no grades of vanity, there are only grades of ability in concealing it."

Mark Twain

"The object of a good general is not to fight, but to win. He has fought enough if he gains a victory."

The Duke of Alva

"Virtue is never left to stand alone. He who has it will have neighbours."

Confucius

"Virtue is the roughest way, But proves at night a bed of down."

Sir Henry Wotton

Addresses • Addresses • Addresses • Addresses • Addresses • Addresses • Addresses

V

Name

Name

Name

Name

Name

Name

USEFUL INFORMATION

~ METRIC CONVERSIONS ~

Metric Conversions	multiply by
acres to hectares	0.4047
cubic inches to cubic centimetres	16.39
cubic feet to cubic metres	0.02832
cubic yards to cubic metres	0.7646
cubic inches to litres	0.01639
feet to metres	0.3048
gallons to litres	4.546
grains to grammes	0.0648
inches to centimetres	2.540
miles to kilometres	1.609

Metric Conversions	multiply by
ounces to grammes	28.35
pounds to kilogrammes	0.4536
pounds to grammes	453.6
square inches to square centimetres	6.452
square feet to square metres	0.0929
square yards to square metres	0.8361
square miles to square kilometres	2.590
tons to kilogrammes	1016.00
yards to metres	0.9144

~ CLOTHING SIZES ~

Men's Suits & Overcoats

American	36	38	40	42	44	46
British	36	38	40	42	44	46
European	46	48	51	54	56	59

Women's Suits & Dresses

American	8	10	12	14	16	18
British	10	12	14	16	18	20
European	38	40	42	44	46	48

Shirts

American	14	14½	15	15½	16	16½	17
British	14	14½	15	15½	16	16½	17
European	36	37	38	39	41	42	43

Men's Shoes

American	7½	8	8½	9½	10½	11½
British	7	7½	8	9	10	11
European	40½	41	42	43	44½	46

Women's Shoes

American	6	6½	7	7½	8	8½
British	4½	5	5½	6	6½	7
European	37½	38	39	39½	40	40½

Children's Clothes

American	4	6	8	10	12	14
British [Height (in)]	43	48	55	58	60	62
European [Height (in)]	109	122	140	147	152	157

Note: Size equivalents are approximate.

EVERYDAY THOUGHTS
for everyday living

"Mankind must put an end to war or war will put an end to mankind."

John F Kennedy

"There never was a good war or a bad peace."

Benjamin Franklin

"Wealthy people miss one of life's great thrills - making the last car payment."

Author Unidentified

"You are as welcome as the flowers in May."

Charles Macklin

"The wisest man sometimes acts weakly, and the weakest sometimes wisely."

Lord Chesterfield

"Wisdom is always an overmatch for strength."

Phaedrus

Addresses • Addresses • Addresses • Addresses • Addresses • Addresses • Addresses • Addresses

W

Name

Name

Name

Name

Name

Name

WEIGHTS & MEASURES

Length

1 centimetre (cm)	=	0.3937 in		
1 metre (m)	=	100 cm	=	1.0936 yds
1 kilometre (km)	=	1000 m	=	0,6214 mile
1 inch	=	2.5400 cm		
1 yard	=	36 in	=	0.9144 m
1 mile	=	1760 yds	=	1.6093 km

Area

1 sq metre (m^2)	=	10 000 cm^2	=	1.1960 sq yds
1 hectare (ha)	=	10 000 m^2	=	2.4711 acres
1 sq km (km^2)	=	100 hectares	=	0.3861 sq mile
1 sq yd	=	9 sq ft	=	0.8361 m^2
1 acre	=	4840 sq yds	=	4046.9 m^2

Capacity

1 cu dm (dm^3)	=	1000 cm^3	=	0.0353 cu ft
1 cu metre (m^3)	=	1000 dm^3	=	1.3080 cu yds
1 litre	=	1 dm^2	=	0.2200 gallon
1 cu yd	=	27 cu ft	=	0.7646 m^3
1 pint	=	4 gills	=	0.5683 litre
1 gallon	=	8 pints	=	4.5461 litres

Weight

1 gramme (g)	=	1000 mg	=	0.3535 oz
1 kilogramme (kg)	=	1000 g	=	2.2046 lb
1 tonne (t)	=	1000 kg	=	0.9842 ton
1 ounce	=	437.5 grains	=	28.350 g
1 pound	=	16 oz	=	0.4536 kg
1 ton	=	2240 pounds	=	1.0161 tonnes

EVERYDAY THOUGHTS
for everyday living

"The seat of knowledge is in the head; of wisdom, in the heart. We are sure to judge wrong if we do not feel right."

William Hazlitt

"It is easier to be wise on behalf of others than to be so for ourselves."

La Rochefoucauld

"The growth of wisdom may be gauged exactly by the dimunition of ill-temper."

Nietzsche

"I never did anything worth doing by accident, nor did any of my inventions come by accident; they came by work."

Thomas A Edison

"The biggest mistake you can make is to believe that you work for someone else."

Author Unidentified

Addresses • Addresses • Addresses • Addresses • Addresses • Addresses • Addresses

W

Name

Name

Name

Name

Name

Name

EMERGENCIES

GAS

IF YOU SMELL GAS

- Put out cigarettes. Do not use matches or naked flames.
- Do not operate electrical switches—either on or off.
- Open doors and windows to let the gas escape.
- Check to see if a tap has been left on accidentally or if a pilot light has gone out.
- If not, there is probably a gas leak. So turn off the whole supply at the meter and call gas service.

ELECTRICITY

POWER CUTS

Make things easier for yourself by planning for power cuts. Keep a good supply of candles, matches, torches and lamps (and fuel) in a place where you can find them easily in the dark. You might consider buying a calor gas or paraffin heater and/or a calor gas camping stove for such instances.

- Switch off lights and electrical appliances such as blankets, fires and cookers as they could cause an accident when the power is switched back on.
- Leave the fridge and freezer switched on, but check that the fridge drip tray is in position and keep the door closed. The freezer contents should remain unharmed for at least 8 hours but it might be an idea to insure your freezer contents anyway.
- Never let children carry candles unless accompanied by an adult. Give them a torch instead.
- When the power is restored remember to extinguish all candles.
- Reset all electric clocks including those which control central heating.

FIRE

WHAT TO DO IF FIRE BREAKS OUT

Remember that smoke can kill as well as flames. If there is smoke, or whenever the fire is too big to tackle quickly and safely:

- Get everyone out of the house at once
- Shut all doors behind you
- Call the Fire Service

If you are trapped in a room

- Keep the door shut.
- Put a blanket or carpet at the bottom of the door.
- Go to the window and call for help.

If you have to escape

- Throw a mattress out of the window and lower yourself out of the window, feet first. Hold on to the sill with your hands and drop onto the mattress.

CHIP PAN FIRES

- Switch off the heat.
- Smother the pan with a large lid or damp cloth.
- Don't move the pan or throw water on it.

ELECTRICAL FIRES

- Switch off at the socket and unplug.
- Never use water while the power is on.
- Use a dry powder extinguisher to put out the fire.

FLOODING

NATURAL DISASTER

Emergency services automatically move into operation when an area is flooded or likely to flood through adverse weather or other natural conditions. Switch off your electricity supply at the mains if it is accessible (make sure your hands are dry), if possible move on to an upper floor and wait for help to arrive.

EVERYDAY THOUGHTS
for everyday living

"Our youth we can have but to-day,
We may always find time to grow old."

George Berkeley

"Youth is a fire, and the years are
a pack of wolves who grow
bolder as the fire dies down."

Author Unidentified

"It is better to waste one's youth
than to do nothing with it at all."

Georges Courteline

"Experience shows that success is due
less to ability than to zeal. The winner
is he who gives himself to his work,
body and soul."

Charles Buxton

"Zeal will do more than knowledge."

William Hazlitt

Name

✉

☎

Name

✉

☎

Name

✉

☎

Name

✉

☎

Name

✉

☎

Name

✉

☎

FIRST AID

The following details are provided by St. John Ambulance. For a thorough knowledge of first aid, look out for courses held by St. John Ambulance, the British Red Cross and St. Andrew's Ambulance Association.

THE ABC OF RESUSCITATION

A Open the Airway

Lift the casualty's jaw and tilt his head to open the airway. Carefully remove any obvious debris from inside his mouth.

B Check Breathing

Look to see if his chest is rising and falling. Listen and feel for breath against your cheek.

C Circulation – Check the Pulse

Find the pulse in his neck by placing your fingers to the side of his voicebox and pressing gently down.

If pulse and breathing are both present . . .

Turn the casualty into the recovery position.

If there is a pulse but no breathing . . .

Start artificial ventilation. If you must leave him to send for an ambulance, give 10 breaths before going and return quickly to continue.

If there is no pulse and no breathing . . .

Phone for an ambulance, then start chest compressions combined with ventilations.

EMERGENCY AID *

Artificial Ventilation

Pinch casualty's nose firmly.

Take a deep breath and seal your lips around casualty's lips then blow into his mouth watching his chest rise. Let his chest fall completely.

Continue at about 10 breaths a minute, checking the pulse after every 10 breaths.

When breathing starts, turn him into the recovery position.

Chest Compression

Give 2 breaths of artificial ventilation. Place the heel of your hand 2 fingers breadth above the junction of rib margin and breastbone. Place your other hand on top and interlock fingers. Keeping your arms straight press down 4-5 cm (1½-2"), 15 times at a rate of 80 per minute. Repeat cycle (2 breaths to 15 compressions). If condition improves, check the pulse.

RECOVERY POSITION

Turn the casualty onto his side. Keep his head tilted with his jaw forward to maintain the open airway. Check that he cannot roll forwards or backwards. Check his breathing and pulse frequently. If they stop follow the ABC of resuscitation.

CHOKING

A foreign object sticking at the back of the throat may block the throat or induce muscular spasm.

Look out for:

Difficulty in breathing and speaking; blueness of the skin; signs from the casualty – pointing to the throat, or grasping the neck

Your aim is:

To remove the obstruction and restore normal breathing

* *Never practise on healthy people.*

JANUARY PLANNER

1
2
3
4
5
6
7
8
9
10
11
12
13
14
15
16
17
18
19
20
21
22
23
24
25
26
27
28
29
30
31

FEBRUARY PLANNER

1
2
3
4
5
6
7
8
9
10
11
12
13
14
15
16
17
18
19
20
21
22
23
24
25
26
27
28
29

For an Adult

1. Bend the casualty well forwards and give five sharp slaps between the shoulder blades.
2. If this fails, try abdominal thrusts. The obstruction may be expelled by the sudden pull against the diaphragm.
3. Continue with back slaps and abdominal thrusts alternately.
4. If the casualty becomes unconscious, lay him face down upon the floor. Kneel astride him and perform abdominal thrusts.

If breathing returns, place the patient in the recovery position and call for an ambulance. If it does not, dial 999 for an ambulance and begin resuscitation.

For a Casualty who Becomes Unconscious

1. Loss of consciousness may relieve muscle spasm, so check first to see if the casualty can now breath. If not, turn him on his side and give 4-5 blows beneath his shoulderblades.
2. If back blows fail, kneel astride the casualty and perform abdominal thrusts.

If he starts to breathe normally, place in the recovery position and call an ambulance. Check and record breathing and pulse rate every 10 minutes.

If he does not start to breathe again, dial 999 for an ambulance and begin resuscitation.

FAINTING

A faint may be a reaction to pain or fright, of the result of emotional upset, exhaustion, or lack of food. It is most common after long periods of physical inactivity, especially in warm atmospheres. Blood pools in the lower part of the body, reducing the amount available to the brain. Recovery from fainting is usually rapid and complete.

Look out for:

A brief loss of consciousness, a slow pulse and pallor

Your aim is:

To improve blood flow to the brain; to reassure the casualty as he recovers, and to make him comfortable

1. Lay the casualty down, and raise and support his legs.
2. Make sure he has plenty of fresh air: open a window if necessary.
3. As he recovers, reassure him and help him sit up gradually.
4. Look for and treat any injury sustained through falling.

If he does not regain consciousness quickly, check breathing and pulse, and be prepared to resuscitate if necessary. Place in the recovery position and call for an ambulance.

If he starts to feel faint again, place his head between his knees and tell him to take deep breaths.

FOREIGN BODIES IN THE SKIN

Your aim is:

To remove the splinter if it protrudes from the skin and to minimise the risk of infection

MARCH PLANNER

1
2
3
4
5
6
7
8
9
10
11
12
13
14
15
16
17
18
19
20
21
22
23
24
25
26
27
28
29
30
31

APRIL PLANNER

1
2
3
4
5
6
7
8
9
10
11
12
13
14
15
16
17
18
19
20
21
22
23
24
25
26
27
28
29
30

1. Clean the area around the splinter with soap and warm water. Sterilize a pair of tweezers by passing them through a flame.
2. Grasp the splinter as close to the skin as possible, and draw it out along the tract of its entry.
3. Squeeze the wound to encourage a little bleeding. Clean the area and apply an adhesive dressing.

If the splinter does not come out easily or breaks up, treat as an embedded foreign body. Never probe the area (for example, with a needle).

4. Check that the casualty's tetanus immunisation is up to date. If in doubt, advise the casualty to see his doctor.

FOREIGN BODIES IN THE EYE

Look out for:

Blurred vision, pain, or discomfort; redness and watering of the eye; eyelids screwed up in spasm

Your aim is:

To prevent injury to the eye

Do not touch anything sticking to, or embedded in the eyeball, or on the coloured part of the eye. Cover the affected eye with an eye pad, bandage both eyes, then take or send the casualty to hospital.

If the object is on the white of the eye, and not stuck:

1. Advise the casualty not to rub his eye. Sit him down facing the light.
2. Gently separate the eyelids with your finger and thumb. Examine every part of his eye.
3. If you can see the foreign body, wash it out using a glass or an eye irrigator, and clean water (sterile, if possible).
4. If this is unsuccessful then, providing the foreign body is not stuck in place, lift it off with a moist swab, or the damp corner of a tissue or clean handkerchief.

If the object is under the eyelid, grasping the lashes, pull the upper lid over the lower lid. Blinking the eye under water may also make the object float clear.

FOREIGN BODIES IN THE NOSE

Look out for:

Difficulty in breathing, or noisy breathing, through the nose; swelling of the nose; smelly or blood-stained discharge indicating an object present for some time

Your aim is:

To obtain medical attention

Do not attempt to remove the foreign body - you may cause injury

1. Keep the casualty quiet. Advise him to breathe through the mouth.
2. Take or send the casualty to hospital.

FOREIGN BODIES IN THE EAR

Your aim is:

To prevent injury to the ear and to obtain medical aid if necessary

For a lodged foreign body

Do not attempt to remove the object. You may cause serious injury or push the object in further.

MAY PLANNER

1
2
3
4
5
6
7
8
9
10
11
12
13
14
15
16
17
18
19
20
21
22
23
24
25
26
27
28
29
30
31

JUNE PLANNER

1
2
3
4
5
6
7
8
9
10
11
12
13
14
15
16
17
18
19
20
21
22
23
24
25
26
27
28
29
30

Take or send the casualty to hospital. Reassure him during transport or until help arrives.

For an insect in the ear

1. Sit the casualty down.
2. Gently flood the ear with tepid water so that the insect floats out.
3. If this is unsuccessful, take or send the casualty to hospital.

HOUSEHOLD POISONS

Almost every household contains poisonous substances, such as bleach, paint stripper, glue, paraffin, and weedkiller, which can be spilled, causing chemical burns, or swallowed. Children in particular are at risk from accidental household poisoning.

Preventing Poisoning in the Home

- Keep dangerous chemicals out of children's reach (not under the sink)
- Keep medicines in a locked cupboard
- Leave poisonous household substances in their original containers
- Buy medicines and household substances in tamper-proof containers

Your aim is:

To maintain airway, breathing, and circulation; to obtain medical aid; and to identify the poison

For Chemicals on the Skin

1. Wash away any residual chemical on the skin with plenty of water.
   Do not contaminate yourself with the dangerous chemical or the rinsing water.
2. Use your judgement to call a doctor or dial 999 for an ambulance. Give information about the spilled chemical.

For Swallowed Poisons

1. Check and, if necessary, clear the airway.
   If the casualty is unconscious, check breathing and pulse, and be prepared to resuscitate. If artificial ventilation is necessary, a plastic face shield will protect you if there is burning around the mouth.

Place the casualty in the recovery position: he may well vomit.

Do not try to induce vomiting.

2. Use your judgement to call a doctor or dial 999 for an ambulance. Give information about the swallowed poison.

If a conscious casualty's lips are burned by corrosive substances, give him frequent sips of cold water or milk.

INSECT STINGS

- If the sting is visible, gently remove with tweezers.
- Apply a cold pad, surgical spirit or a solution of bicarbonate of soda.

JULY PLANNER

1
2
3
4
5
6
7
8
9
10
11
12
13
14
15
16
17
18
19
20
21
22
23
24
25
26
27
28
29
30
31

AUGUST PLANNER

1
2
3
4
5
6
7
8
9
10
11
12
13
14
15
16
17
18
19
20
21
22
23
24
25
26
27
28
29
30
31

CHILDHOOD INFECTIONS

	MEASLES	WHOOPING COUGH	MUMPS	CHICKENPOX	GERMAN MEASLES (*Rubella*)	GASTRO-ENTERITIS
INCUBATION PERIOD	8 to 10 days before the running nose and head cold, 14 days before the appearance of the rash.	8 to 14 days.	14 to 28 days.	10 to 25 days.	14 to 21 days.	1 to 7 days; varies with different germs.
EARLY SYMPTOMS	Starts with a running nose, bleary eyes and a hard cough. The doctor will look inside the mouth for minute white spots which appear 2 or 3 days before the rash.	Starts with "chestiness" and a simple cough. This later becomes spasmodic with "paroxysms" ending with a whoop and/or vomiting.	Generally off colour for a few days before they complain of pain or soreness on chewing.	First sign of the illness is usually the detection of spots on the trunk when the child is being bathed or undressed.	Some throat discomfort and slight fever at onset but the appearance of the rash is often the first sign of the disease. Painful swollen glands at the back of the head.	Nausea and vomiting often followed by diarrhoea. There may be fever.
DISTINCTIVE FEATURES	The rash appears 3 or 4 days after the first symptoms and begins behind the ears, spreads to the face and then downwards to the body and lower limbs. It consists of dark, purplish, spots which run together to make blotchy areas. The eyes are always reddened.	When fully developed diagnosis is obvious. Hurried breathing denotes onset of pneumonia. This may occur early in young children who have not been immunised and may leave permanent lung damage. Children with severe or frequent vomiting need more food after a paroxysm..	The salivary gland below the ear and behind the angle of the jaw is swollen and painful on pressure. The gland on the opposite side may be involved up to 7 days later. Boys after puberty may develop painful swelling of the testicles. Mild, transient meningitis is quite common, but it does not usually need special treatment.	The spots become "blistery" then yellow and form scabs. There may be several "crops" of spots.	The rash consists of pink flat spots which merge together to give a "peachbloom" appearance. There is no red throat or pallor round the mouth.	Vomiting rarely lasts more than a day or two, but diarrhoea may persist. Crampy stomach pains are common, but very severe stomach ache, or blood in more than 2 or 3 motions need checking on by the doctor.
DURATION	Allow for a few days in bed and 2 weeks before they can return to school.	A severe attack will require at least 6 weeks before return to school but mild cases sometimes occur in children who have been immunised.	Only severe cases need to be confined to bed. Return to school after the swelling has subsided.	A child is no longer infectious as soon as ALL the spots have dried to scabs.	Uneventful recovery within 6 days. All German Measles patients should be isolated from pregnant women.	Usually 1 to 4 days. Severe cases may last many days. Solid foods need not be given until diarrhoea improves.
NURSING POINTS	The mouth needs special care with mouthwashes or swabbing after food. Shortness of breath as rash fades, persistent severe ear ache and very inflamed eyes usually require medical advice.	The small infant requires special care during paroxysms and should be lifted out of the cot and held head downwards until the spasm ceases. Older children should be calmed and reassured but can cope with their own spasms.	Careful washing of the mouth after a meal is important to remove all crumbs.	It is almost impossible to prevent the child from scratching the irritable spots so fingernails should be kept short.	The course of the disease is usually uneventful. Some patients develop pain and swelling in the small joints of the hands. This will subside.	Babies do best on frequent small breast feeds and plenty of boiled water. Otherwise make up electrolyte powder or tablets (from the chemist) in boiled water. Watered-down fizzy drinks may also be accepted by older children.

SEPTEMBER PLANNER

1
2
3
4
5
6
7
8
9
10
11
12
13
14
15
16
17
18
19
20
21
22
23
24
25
26
27
28
29
30

OCTOBER PLANNER

1
2
3
4
5
6
7
8
9
10
11
12
13
14
15
16
17
18
19
20
21
22
23
24
25
26
27
28
29
30
31

MEDICAL RECORDS

Use this page to keep a note of family medical records, such as dates of vaccinations and boosters.

NOVEMBER PLANNER

1
2
3
4
5
6
7
8
9
10
11
12
13
14
15
16
17
18
19
20
21
22
23
24
25
26
27
28
29
30

DECEMBER PLANNER

1
2
3
4
5
6
7
8
9
10
11
12
13
14
15
16
17
18
19
20
21
22
23
24
25
26
27
28
29
30
31

Name

Name

Name

Name

Name

Name

Name

Name

Name

Name

Name

Name

ame

ame

ame

ame

ame

ame

Name

Name

Name

Name

Name

Name

Name

✉

☎

Name

✉

☎

Name

✉

☎

Name

✉

☎

Name

✉

☎

Name

✉

☎

Name

✉

☎

Name

✉

☎

Name

✉

☎

Name

✉

☎

Name

✉

☎

Name

✉

☎

ame

✉

☎

ame

✉

☎

ame

✉

☎

ame

✉

☎

ame

✉

☎

ame

✉

☎

Name

✉

☎

Name

✉

☎

Name

✉

☎

Name

✉

☎

Name

✉

☎

Name

✉

☎

Name

✉

☎

Name

✉

☎

Name

✉

☎

Name

✉

☎

Name

✉

☎

Name

✉

☎

Name

✉

☎

Name

✉

☎

Name

✉

☎

Name

✉

☎

Name

✉

☎

Name

✉

☎

ame

ame

ame

ame

ame

ame

Name

Name

Name

Name

Name

Name